Introduction to Cybersecurity

1.1 What is Cybersecurity?

1.2 The Importance of Cybersecurity

1.3 Cybersecurity vs. Information Security

1.4 The CIA Triad: Confidentiality, Integrity, and Availability

1.5 Cybersecurity Challenges in the Digital Age

1.6 The Human Factor in Cybersecurity

1.7 The Future of Cybersecurity

Module 1: Fundamentals of Cybersecurity

1.1 Common Cybersecurity Terminology and Concepts

1.2 Types of Cyber Threats and Attack Vectors

1.3 Cybersecurity Frameworks and Standards

1.4 Risk Management and Security Controls

1.5 Securing Networks and Infrastructure

1.6 Securing Data and Information

1.7 User Authentication and Access Control

1.8 Security Awareness and Training

Module 2: Network Security

2.1 Network Architecture and Design

2.2 Firewalls and Intrusion Detection Systems (IDS)

2.3 Virtual Private Networks (VPNs) and Secure Socket Layer (SSL)

2.4 Wireless Network Security

2.5 Network Monitoring and Incident Response

Module 3: Operating System Security

3.1 Securing Operating Systems (Windows, macOS, Linux)

3.2 Patch Management and Software Updates

3.3 Host-based Intrusion Detection and Prevention

3.4 Securing Mobile Devices

Module 4: Application Security

4.1 Web Application Security

4.2 Secure Coding Practices

4.3 Input Validation and Output Encoding

4.4 Security Testing and Code Review

4.5 Application Security Tools

Module 5: Cloud Security
5.1 Cloud Computing Models and Deployment Models
5.2 Securing Cloud Environments
5.3 Cloud Identity and Access Management
5.4 Data Security in the Cloud

Module 6: Cryptography
6.1 Introduction to Cryptography
6.2 Symmetric and Asymmetric Encryption
6.3 Public Key Infrastructure (PKI)
6.4 Digital Signatures and Certificates
6.5 Cryptographic Attacks and Countermeasures

Module 7: Incident Response and Cyber Forensics
7.1 Incident Response Process and Best Practices
7.2 Cyber Forensics Techniques
7.3 Preservation and Analysis of Digital Evidence

7.4 Legal and Ethical Considerations in Cyber Forensics

Module 8: Ethical Hacking and Penetration Testing
8.1 Introduction to Ethical Hacking
8.2 Penetration Testing Methodologies
8.3 Exploiting Vulnerabilities and Vulnerability Assessment
8.4 Reporting and Mitigating Security Findings

Module 9: Cybersecurity for Internet of Things (IoT)
9.1 IoT Architecture and Security Challenges
9.2 Securing IoT Devices and Communications
9.3 Privacy and Data Protection in IoT
9.4 IoT Security Best Practices

Module 10: Cybersecurity Governance and Compliance
10.1 Creating Cybersecurity Policies and Procedures

Introduction to Cybersecurity

1.1 What is Cybersecurity?

Cybersecurity is the practice of protecting computers, servers, networks, data, and other digital systems from unauthorized access, attacks, damage, and theft. It encompasses a set of measures, technologies, processes, and best practices designed to safeguard information technology (IT) assets and ensure the confidentiality, integrity, and availability of data and services.

The primary goal of cybersecurity is to defend against cyber threats, which can include various malicious activities such as hacking, malware infections, phishing attacks, ransomware, denial-of-service (DoS) attacks, and more. Cybersecurity professionals work to identify vulnerabilities, implement security measures, monitor systems for potential threats, and respond swiftly and effectively to security incidents.

Key elements of cybersecurity include network security, data protection, access controls, encryption, authentication mechanisms, security awareness training for users, incident response, and cybersecurity governance. Cybersecurity is a critical aspect of modern society, as it plays a significant role in safeguarding individuals, businesses, governments, and organizations from cybercrimes and cyber-espionage, contributing to the overall stability and trust in the digital ecosystem.

1.2 The Importance of Cybersecurity

The importance of cybersecurity cannot be overstated in today's digital world. Here are some key reasons why cybersecurity is of utmost significance:

1. Protecting Confidentiality: Cybersecurity ensures that sensitive information remains

confidential and is accessible only to authorized individuals. This includes personal data, financial records, intellectual property, and classified government information.

2. Safeguarding Integrity: Cybersecurity measures prevent unauthorized alteration or tampering of data, ensuring that information remains accurate and reliable. Maintaining data integrity is vital in critical systems such as healthcare, finance, and critical infrastructure.

3. Ensuring Availability: Cybersecurity helps maintain the availability of digital systems and services. DDoS attacks and other cyber threats can disrupt services, leading to financial losses, inconvenience, and potential safety risks.

4. Protecting Personal Privacy: Cybersecurity safeguards individuals' online privacy and prevents the unauthorized collection and misuse of personal data by cybercriminals.

5. Preventing Financial Losses: Cyberattacks can lead to significant financial losses for individuals and organizations. Cybersecurity helps prevent data breaches, ransomware attacks, and fraud, mitigating financial risks.

6. Preserving Business Reputation: A cybersecurity breach can severely damage an organization's reputation and trust among customers, partners, and stakeholders. By implementing robust cybersecurity measures, businesses can demonstrate their commitment to protecting sensitive data.

7. National Security: Cybersecurity is crucial for safeguarding a country's national security interests, including protecting government networks, infrastructure, and sensitive data from cyber threats and cyber-espionage.

8. Countering Cybercrime: Cybersecurity efforts help in detecting, investigating, and

prosecuting cybercriminals, making the internet a safer place for everyone.

9. Supporting Digital Innovation: A secure digital environment fosters innovation and enables the adoption of emerging technologies, such as the Internet of Things (IoT), cloud computing, and artificial intelligence.

10. Protecting Critical Infrastructure: Cybersecurity is vital for safeguarding essential services such as power grids, transportation systems, healthcare facilities, and emergency services from cyber threats that could have catastrophic consequences.

1.3 Cybersecurity vs. Information Security

Cybersecurity and information security are related concepts, but they have distinct scopes and areas of focus within the broader domain of security. Here's a comparison of the two:

Cybersecurity:
- Cybersecurity primarily deals with protecting digital systems, networks, and data from cyber threats and attacks in the digital realm. It focuses on securing information and communication technologies (ICT) and the internet against malicious activities.
- The term "cyber" refers to anything related to the internet and digital technology.
- Cybersecurity measures include safeguarding computers, servers, network devices, and cloud infrastructure from cyber threats like hacking, malware, phishing, ransomware, and denial-of-service (DoS) attacks.

- It involves defending against external threats that originate from the internet or connected devices.

Information Security:
- Information security, on the other hand, is a broader discipline that encompasses protecting all forms of information, regardless of its format, both digital and non-digital. It includes physical documents, intellectual property, trade secrets, and classified data, among others.
- Information security is not limited to the digital realm but also covers physical security measures to protect physical assets.
- Information security measures include controlling access to information, ensuring data confidentiality, preventing unauthorized modification, and maintaining data integrity across various forms of data storage.
- It involves safeguarding information regardless of where it resides, such as in physical filing cabinets, data centers, cloud storage, or on networked devices.

1.4 The CIA Triad: Confidentiality, Integrity, and Availability

The CIA Triad is a foundational concept in information security and cybersecurity, representing the three essential principles that guide the design and implementation of secure systems. The acronym CIA stands for Confidentiality, Integrity, and Availability. These principles work together to ensure that information and data are adequately protected and accessible only to authorized users. Let's explore each component of the CIA Triad:

1. Confidentiality:
Confidentiality refers to the protection of sensitive information from unauthorized access or disclosure. It ensures that data is only accessible to those with the appropriate permissions or clearance. Maintaining confidentiality helps prevent unauthorized

individuals or entities from gaining access to sensitive data, thereby protecting privacy and sensitive information.

Confidentiality measures include:

- Access controls: Implementing user authentication mechanisms, like passwords or multi-factor authentication, to verify the identity of users before granting access to sensitive data.
- Encryption: Transforming data into an unreadable format (cipher) to prevent unauthorized users from understanding the information without the proper decryption key.
- Data classification: Categorizing data based on its sensitivity and applying different access controls and protection measures accordingly.

2. Integrity:

Integrity ensures that data remains accurate, reliable, and unaltered throughout its lifecycle. It involves protecting data from unauthorized modifications, deletions, or tampering. Maintaining data integrity is crucial in critical systems where accuracy and consistency are paramount.

Integrity measures include:

- Data validation: Implementing input validation and verification mechanisms to ensure that data is accurate and free from errors.
- Digital signatures: Applying cryptographic techniques to sign data or files to detect unauthorized changes.
- Version control: Implementing processes to manage and track changes made to data, ensuring accountability and traceability.

3. Availability:

Availability ensures that information and systems are accessible and usable by authorized users when needed. It involves preventing or minimizing downtime, ensuring that services and resources are continuously available for legitimate users.

Availability measures include:

- Redundancy: Implementing backup systems, failover mechanisms, and redundant components to ensure continuous service availability in case of failures.
- Load balancing: Distributing network traffic across multiple servers or resources to prevent overload and ensure optimal performance.
- Disaster recovery planning: Developing plans and procedures to recover from system failures, natural disasters, or cyber attacks and restore operations promptly.

The CIA Triad serves as a fundamental framework for designing secure systems, providing a comprehensive approach to protect information and systems from a wide range of threats. By addressing the principles of confidentiality, integrity, and availability, organizations can establish a robust security posture and mitigate potential risks effectively.

1.5 Cybersecurity Challenges in the Digital Age

In the digital age, cybersecurity faces numerous challenges due to the increasing reliance on technology and the complexity of cyber threats. Some of the significant cybersecurity challenges include:

1. Evolving Cyber Threat Landscape: Cyber threats are constantly evolving, becoming

more sophisticated, and harder to detect. Cybercriminals use advanced techniques, such as artificial intelligence and automation, to launch targeted attacks on individuals, businesses, and governments.

2. Data Breaches and Privacy Concerns: Data breaches continue to be a significant cybersecurity challenge, exposing sensitive information of individuals and organizations. The loss of personal data raises privacy concerns and can lead to financial fraud or identity theft.

3. Ransomware and Extortion Attacks: Ransomware attacks have become increasingly prevalent, where cybercriminals encrypt valuable data and demand ransom payments for decryption keys. Such attacks can cripple businesses and result in substantial financial losses.

4. Insider Threats: Insider threats, where employees or trusted individuals

intentionally or unintentionally compromise security, pose a significant challenge. Insider attacks can be difficult to detect and prevent, as insiders often have legitimate access to sensitive information.

5. IoT and Smart Devices Vulnerabilities: The proliferation of Internet of Things (IoT) devices introduces new attack surfaces and vulnerabilities. Inadequate security measures in smart devices can lead to large-scale cyberattacks, affecting critical infrastructure and public safety.

6. Cloud Security Risks: As cloud computing gains popularity, concerns about the security of data stored in the cloud increase. Misconfigurations, data breaches, and unauthorized access are among the top cloud security challenges.

7. Lack of Cybersecurity Skills: There is a shortage of skilled cybersecurity professionals to meet the growing demand

for protecting digital systems. This scarcity hampers organizations' abilities to build and maintain strong cybersecurity defenses.

8. Zero-Day Exploits: Zero-day exploits are vulnerabilities unknown to software developers, making them challenging to defend against until patches are released. Attackers can exploit these vulnerabilities to launch targeted attacks.

9. Social Engineering and Phishing: Social engineering techniques, such as phishing emails and social media scams, continue to be successful in tricking users into divulging sensitive information or clicking on malicious links.

10. Global Cyber Espionage and State-Sponsored Attacks: Nation-states engage in cyber espionage and cyber warfare to gather intelligence, disrupt adversaries, and assert dominance in the digital realm. These attacks

can have severe implications for national security.

11. Compliance and Regulatory Challenges: Compliance with cybersecurity regulations and standards presents challenges for businesses, as regulations differ across regions and industries.

Addressing these challenges requires a multi-layered and proactive approach to cybersecurity. Organizations and individuals must stay vigilant, implement robust security measures, conduct regular risk assessments, and invest in cybersecurity awareness and education to combat the ever-evolving cyber threats in the digital age.

1.6 The Human Factor in Cybersecurity

The human factor in cybersecurity refers to the role that individuals play in both the vulnerability and defense of digital systems and data. It recognizes that human behavior, actions, and decisions can significantly impact the security posture of organizations and individuals in the context of cybersecurity.

Here are some key aspects of the human factor in cybersecurity:

1. User Awareness and Training: Users, whether employees or individuals, are often the first line of defense against cyber threats. Raising cybersecurity awareness through training programs helps users recognize and respond appropriately to phishing attempts, social engineering attacks, and other security risks.

2. Insider Threats: Insider threats occur when employees or trusted individuals within an organization intentionally or unintentionally compromise security. These threats may involve data theft, sabotage, or unauthorized access to sensitive information.

3. Social Engineering: Cybercriminals often exploit human psychology through social engineering techniques to manipulate users into divulging sensitive information or taking actions that compromise security. Phishing, pretexting, and baiting are common social engineering tactics.

4. Password Security: Weak passwords and poor password management practices are a significant vulnerability in cybersecurity. Encouraging users to adopt strong and unique passwords and implementing multi-factor authentication can mitigate this risk.

5. Human Error: Mistakes made by employees, such as clicking on malicious links or inadvertently disclosing sensitive information, can lead to security breaches. Comprehensive training and ongoing awareness efforts can reduce the likelihood of such errors.

6. BYOD (Bring Your Own Device) Policies: The use of personal devices for work purposes can introduce security risks if not adequately managed. Proper policies and security measures are essential to secure personal devices used in a professional setting.

7. Phishing and Spear Phishing: Phishing attacks often target individuals through emails, messages, or phone calls. Educating users about these threats and how to identify suspicious communications is crucial.

8. Security Culture: Fostering a security-aware culture within organizations promotes a collective responsibility for cybersecurity. When cybersecurity becomes an integral part of the organization's values, employees are more likely to be vigilant and report potential security incidents.

9. Mobile Devices and Remote Work: The rise of mobile devices and remote work has

increased the surface area for potential cyber threats. Proper security practices for remote work and mobile devices are essential to mitigate risks.

10. Cybersecurity Education for Children: As children increasingly use digital devices, providing cybersecurity education at a young age can instill safe online behaviors and protect them from potential risks.

1.7 The Future of Cybersecurity

The future of cybersecurity promises to be dynamic and challenging, driven by the rapid evolution of technology and the ever-changing cyber threat landscape. Here are some key trends and areas that are likely to shape the future of cybersecurity:

1. Artificial Intelligence (AI) and Machine Learning: AI and machine learning will play an increasingly significant role in cybersecurity. They will be used for threat detection, anomaly detection, pattern recognition, and automated response to cyber threats, enabling faster and more efficient cybersecurity operations.

2. Quantum Computing and Encryption: The emergence of quantum computing may pose challenges to traditional encryption methods. However, it also presents opportunities to develop quantum-resistant encryption algorithms to protect sensitive data against quantum attacks.

3. Internet of Things (IoT) Security: As the number of connected devices continues to grow, securing the IoT ecosystem will become critical. Ensuring the security and

privacy of IoT devices and their communications will be a top priority to prevent large-scale cyber-attacks.

4. Cloud Security: With the widespread adoption of cloud computing, securing cloud environments will remain a focus area. Advanced cloud security solutions and best practices will be essential to protect data and applications in the cloud.

5. Cyber-Physical Systems (CPS) Security: As industries rely more on interconnected cyber-physical systems, ensuring the security of critical infrastructure, smart cities, and industrial control systems will be crucial to prevent potential disruptions and physical harm.

6. Zero-Trust Architecture: Zero-trust security models, which assume that no user or device should be inherently trusted, will gain traction. Implementing zero-trust architectures will enhance security posture

by enforcing strict access controls and verification at all levels.

7. Biometrics and Advanced Authentication: Biometric authentication, such as fingerprint scanning and facial recognition, will become more prevalent for secure user authentication. Advancements in biometrics and behavioral analytics will improve user identification and fraud detection.

8. Privacy and Data Protection Regulations: Privacy regulations will continue to evolve and impact how organizations handle and protect user data. Compliance with privacy laws, such as GDPR and CCPA, will be essential for businesses to maintain consumer trust.

9. Cybersecurity Workforce Development: The shortage of skilled cybersecurity professionals will continue to be a challenge. Efforts to bridge this gap through training, education, and workforce development

initiatives will be crucial to meet the growing demand for cybersecurity experts.

10. AI-Driven Cyber Threats: Cybercriminals will increasingly use AI to launch more sophisticated and targeted attacks. Defending against AI-driven threats will require advanced cybersecurity solutions and AI-based security measures.

Module 1: Fundamentals of Cybersecurity

1.1 Common Cybersecurity Terminology and Concepts

Understanding common cybersecurity terminology and concepts is essential for anyone involved in information security. Here are some key terms and concepts:

1. Threat: Any potential danger or harmful event that can exploit a vulnerability in a system or network, leading to security breaches or attacks.

2. Vulnerability: A weakness or flaw in a system or network that can be exploited by a threat, potentially resulting in a security breach.

3. Risk: The probability of a threat exploiting a vulnerability and the potential impact or consequences of a successful attack.

4. Attack: An intentional and malicious attempt to exploit a vulnerability in a system or network, aiming to compromise its security.

5. Malware: Malicious software designed to harm, steal data, or gain unauthorized access to computer systems. Types include viruses, worms, Trojans, ransomware, and spyware.

6. Phishing: A social engineering attack where attackers deceive users into revealing sensitive information, often through emails, messages, or fake websites.

7. Social Engineering: Manipulative techniques used by attackers to trick individuals into disclosing sensitive information or taking certain actions.

8. Firewall: A security system that monitors and controls network traffic based on predefined rules to prevent unauthorized access and block malicious activity.

9. Intrusion Detection System (IDS): A security tool that monitors network traffic and system activity to identify suspicious behavior or potential security breaches.

10. Intrusion Prevention System (IPS): An advanced security tool that not only detects but also actively blocks and mitigates potential cyber threats.

11. Encryption: The process of converting data into a secure and unreadable format using cryptographic algorithms to protect

sensitive information from unauthorized access.

12. Authentication: Verifying the identity of users or devices trying to access a system, often through usernames, passwords, biometrics, or multi-factor authentication.

13. Authorization: The process of granting specific privileges and access rights to authenticated users based on their roles and responsibilities.

14. Patch Management: Regularly updating software and systems with security patches to fix known vulnerabilities and improve overall security.

15. Two-Factor Authentication (2FA): A security mechanism that requires users to provide two different forms of identification to access a system or account, increasing security.

16. Multi-Factor Authentication (MFA): Similar to 2FA but requires users to provide more than two forms of identification for enhanced security.

17. Security Incident: Any event that could potentially lead to a security breach or violation of security policies.

18. Data Breach: Unauthorized access, acquisition, or disclosure of sensitive or confidential information.

19. Denial of Service (DoS) Attack: An attack that aims to make a network or system unavailable to its users by overwhelming it with excessive traffic or requests.

20. Penetration Testing: A controlled and authorized simulation of a cyberattack on a system or network to identify vulnerabilities and weaknesses.

These are just a few of the many cybersecurity terms and concepts that are crucial to understanding and addressing the challenges in the ever-evolving world of information security.

1.2 Types of Cyber Threats and Attack Vectors

Cyber threats and attack vectors are numerous and constantly evolving. Understanding these threats is essential for developing effective cybersecurity strategies. Here are some common types of cyber threats and attack vectors:

1. Malware:
- Viruses: Malicious programs that attach themselves to legitimate files and spread when the infected file is executed.
- Worms: Self-replicating malware that spreads across networks and systems without user interaction.

- Trojans: Disguised as legitimate software, Trojans trick users into installing them, giving attackers unauthorized access to the system.
- Ransomware: Encrypts files or locks users out of their systems, demanding a ransom to restore access.
- Spyware: Stealthily monitors user activities, collecting sensitive information without their knowledge.

2. Phishing and Social Engineering:
- Phishing: Fraudulent attempts to deceive users into divulging sensitive information through emails, messages, or fake websites.
- Spear Phishing: Targeted phishing attacks that tailor messages to specific individuals or organizations.
- Whaling: Phishing attacks specifically targeting high-profile individuals, such as executives or celebrities.

3. Denial of Service (DoS) and Distributed Denial of Service (DDoS) Attacks:

- DoS: Overloads a target system or network with excessive traffic, causing it to become unavailable to users.
- DDoS: Conducted from multiple sources to overwhelm a target with traffic, making it difficult to mitigate.

4. Man-in-the-Middle (MitM) Attack:
- Intercepts communication between two parties to eavesdrop, alter messages, or steal sensitive information.

5. SQL Injection:
- Exploits vulnerabilities in web applications to manipulate database queries and gain unauthorized access to data.

6. Zero-Day Exploits:
- Target vulnerabilities unknown to software vendors, allowing attackers to exploit systems before patches are available.

7. Advanced Persistent Threats (APTs):

- Sophisticated and long-term attacks conducted by well-funded and organized threat actors to steal data or conduct espionage.

8. Insider Threats:
- Malicious or unintentional actions by employees or trusted individuals that compromise security.

9. Internet of Things (IoT) Vulnerabilities:
- Exploiting security weaknesses in connected devices to gain unauthorized access to networks or conduct attacks.

10. Supply Chain Attacks:
- Targeting vulnerabilities in the supply chain to compromise software or hardware before it reaches end-users.

11. Watering Hole Attacks:
- Compromising websites frequented by a target group to infect visitors with malware.

12. Fileless Malware:
- Executes malicious code directly in memory, making it difficult for traditional antivirus software to detect.

13. Credential Stuffing:
- Using stolen username and password combinations to gain unauthorized access to multiple accounts.

These are just a few examples of the many cyber threats and attack vectors prevalent in today's digital landscape. Cybersecurity professionals must remain vigilant and continuously update their defenses to combat these evolving threats effectively.

1.3 Cybersecurity Frameworks and Standards

Cybersecurity frameworks and standards provide organizations with guidelines, best practices, and a structured approach to managing cybersecurity risks and implementing robust security measures. These frameworks help organizations develop comprehensive cybersecurity programs to protect their systems, data, and users. Some of the widely recognized cybersecurity frameworks and standards include:

1. NIST Cybersecurity Framework (NIST CSF): Developed by the National Institute of Standards and Technology (NIST) in the United States, this framework offers a risk-based approach to managing cybersecurity. It consists of five core functions: Identify, Protect, Detect, Respond, and Recover.

2. ISO/IEC 27001:
The International Organization for Standardization (ISO) and the International Electrotechnical Commission (IEC) developed this standard to provide requirements for establishing, implementing, maintaining, and

continually improving an information security management system (ISMS).

3. CIS Controls (Center for Internet Security):
The CIS Controls provide a prioritized set of actions designed to mitigate the most common cyber threats and attacks. The controls are practical, actionable, and easy to implement.

4. PCI DSS (Payment Card Industry Data Security Standard):
PCI DSS is a set of security standards designed to protect credit cardholder data during payment card transactions. It is mandated by the major credit card companies and applies to organizations handling cardholder data.

5. GDPR (General Data Protection Regulation):

The European Union's GDPR is a comprehensive data protection regulation that governs how organizations handle and protect personal data of EU citizens. Compliance is mandatory for organizations processing EU citizen data.

6. HIPAA (Health Insurance Portability and Accountability Act):
HIPAA is a U.S. regulation that sets standards for the security and privacy of protected health information (PHI) in the healthcare industry.

7. FISMA (Federal Information Security Management Act):
FISMA is a U.S. federal law that mandates the implementation of information security controls in federal agencies to protect sensitive information and information systems.

8. COBIT (Control Objectives for Information and Related Technologies):

COBIT is an IT management framework that provides guidance on aligning IT with business goals and managing information risk and security.

9. NIST Risk Management Framework (NIST RMF):

NIST RMF is a systematic process for managing cybersecurity and privacy risk in federal information systems.

10. CSA (Cloud Security Alliance) Security Guidance:

CSA provides a comprehensive guide to cloud security best practices for organizations using or considering cloud services.

1.4 Risk Management and Security Controls

Risk management and security controls are essential components of an effective cybersecurity strategy. They work together to identify potential risks, implement measures to mitigate those risks, and enhance the overall security posture of an organization. Here's an overview of risk management and security controls:

Risk Management:
1. Risk Identification: The process of identifying potential threats, vulnerabilities, and assets within an organization that may be susceptible to cybersecurity risks.

2. Risk Assessment: Evaluating the likelihood and potential impact of identified risks to prioritize and understand their significance.

3. Risk Analysis: Analyzing the data collected during risk assessment to determine the level of risk and develop appropriate risk treatment plans.

4. Risk Treatment: Developing strategies to address identified risks, including risk avoidance, risk reduction, risk transfer, or risk acceptance.

5. Risk Mitigation: Implementing security measures and controls to reduce the likelihood and impact of identified risks.

6. Risk Monitoring and Review: Continuously monitoring the effectiveness of risk treatment plans and reviewing risk assessments regularly to adapt to changing threats.

Security Controls:
1. Administrative Controls: Policies, procedures, and guidelines that govern an organization's security practices, including security policies, access controls, and security awareness training for employees.

2. Technical Controls: Technological measures implemented to safeguard

systems, data, and networks. Examples include firewalls, encryption, intrusion detection systems, and multi-factor authentication.

3. Physical Controls: Physical measures put in place to protect physical assets, such as data centers, servers, and sensitive documents. Examples include access control systems, biometric authentication, and video surveillance.

4. Preventive Controls: Controls designed to prevent security incidents from occurring. They focus on keeping threats at bay and reducing the likelihood of successful attacks.

5. Detective Controls: Controls that identify and detect security incidents or breaches that have already occurred, allowing for a timely response and investigation.

6. Corrective Controls: Measures implemented after a security incident to

mitigate the impact, restore affected systems, and prevent future occurrences.

1.5 Securing Networks and Infrastructure

Securing networks and infrastructure is a critical aspect of cybersecurity, as networks serve as the backbone of communication and data exchange within organizations. Here are some essential steps and best practices for securing networks and infrastructure:

1. Network Segmentation: Divide the network into smaller, isolated segments to limit the impact of a security breach and control the flow of data and access.

2. Perimeter Security: Implement firewalls, intrusion prevention systems (IPS), and demilitarized zones (DMZ) to control and monitor traffic entering and leaving the network.

3. Access Controls: Enforce strong authentication mechanisms, such as multi-factor authentication (MFA), to ensure that only authorized users can access the network and its resources.

4. Network Monitoring: Employ network monitoring and security information and event management (SIEM) tools to detect and respond to suspicious activities and potential security incidents.

5. Patch Management: Regularly update software, firmware, and network devices with the latest security patches to address known vulnerabilities.

6. Network Encryption: Use encryption protocols (such as SSL/TLS) to protect data transmitted over the network, particularly for sensitive information and login credentials.

7. Wireless Network Security: Secure Wi-Fi networks with strong encryption (WPA3), unique passwords, and proper authentication methods to prevent unauthorized access.

8. Network Security Policies: Develop and enforce comprehensive network security policies, including acceptable use policies, password policies, and data handling guidelines.

9. Network Auditing and Testing: Conduct regular network audits and vulnerability assessments to identify potential weaknesses and ensure compliance with security standards.

10. Redundancy and Disaster Recovery: Implement redundant network infrastructure and disaster recovery plans to maintain network availability in case of failures or cyber-attacks.

11. Intrusion Detection and Prevention: Deploy intrusion detection systems (IDS) and intrusion prevention systems (IPS) to identify and block suspicious network activities.

12. Network Access Monitoring: Monitor network access logs to identify unauthorized access attempts and potential security breaches.

13. Network Traffic Analysis: Analyze network traffic patterns to identify anomalies and potential signs of malicious activities.

14. Vendor Security: Ensure that third-party vendors and partners connecting to your network follow robust security practices to prevent supply chain attacks.

15. Employee Awareness: Educate employees about network security best practices, such as identifying phishing emails

and being cautious about connecting to unknown networks.

1.6 Securing Data and Information

Securing data and information is paramount in today's digital world, where sensitive information is a prime target for cybercriminals. Here are some essential steps and best practices to secure data and information effectively:

1. Data Classification: Categorize data based on its sensitivity and criticality to implement appropriate security controls. Differentiate between public, internal, confidential, and classified data.

2. Encryption: Use strong encryption algorithms to protect data both in transit and at rest. This ensures that even if unauthorized individuals gain access to the

data, they cannot decipher it without the encryption keys.

3. Access Controls: Implement granular access controls, assigning appropriate permissions to users based on their roles and responsibilities. Use the principle of least privilege to limit access to data to only those who need it for their work.

4. Multi-Factor Authentication (MFA): Require multi-factor authentication for accessing sensitive information and critical systems. MFA adds an extra layer of security beyond passwords, reducing the risk of unauthorized access.

5. Data Loss Prevention (DLP): Deploy DLP solutions to monitor and prevent sensitive data from being transmitted or shared outside authorized channels. DLP helps detect and block unauthorized data exfiltration attempts.

6. Secure Data Storage: Use secure and encrypted storage solutions, such as encrypted hard drives and cloud storage with encryption features, to safeguard data at rest.

7. Regular Backups: Implement regular and secure data backups to prevent data loss due to hardware failures, ransomware attacks, or accidental deletions.

8. Secure Data Sharing: Use secure file transfer protocols and platforms for sharing sensitive information with authorized recipients.

9. Employee Training: Educate employees about data security best practices, the importance of data protection, and the risks of data breaches caused by human error.

10. Data Retention Policies: Develop and enforce data retention policies to ensure that data is retained only for as long as

necessary and securely disposed of when no longer needed.

11. Secure File Transfer: Use secure file transfer protocols (e.g., SFTP, HTTPS) and encrypted email when transmitting sensitive data externally.

12. Regular Vulnerability Assessments: Conduct regular vulnerability assessments and penetration testing to identify weaknesses in data security and address them promptly.

13. Data Masking and Anonymization: Mask sensitive data in non-production environments to reduce the risk of data exposure during development and testing.

14. Data Privacy Compliance: Ensure compliance with relevant data privacy regulations, such as GDPR, CCPA, HIPAA, and others, to protect individuals' privacy rights and avoid legal consequences.

15. Incident Response Plan: Develop a comprehensive incident response plan to address data breaches or security incidents promptly and effectively.

1.7 User Authentication and Access Control

User authentication and access control are crucial components of a secure information system, ensuring that only authorized individuals have access to sensitive data and resources. Let's delve into each of these concepts:

1. User Authentication:
User authentication is the process of verifying the identity of a user attempting to access a system, application, or network. It ensures that only legitimate users with the correct credentials can gain entry. There are several methods of user authentication:

- Password-based authentication: Users provide a username and password to prove their identity.
- Multi-Factor Authentication (MFA): Requires users to provide two or more authentication factors, such as something they know (password), something they have (smartphone or hardware token), or something they are (fingerprint or facial recognition).
- Biometric authentication: Uses physical characteristics like fingerprints, retina scans, or facial recognition to verify a user's identity.
- Single Sign-On (SSO): Allows users to access multiple applications and services with a single set of credentials, streamlining the authentication process and enhancing user experience.

2. Access Control:
Access control refers to the mechanisms and policies that regulate user access to specific data, systems, or resources within an

organization. It ensures that users only have access to the resources they need to perform their roles and responsibilities, following the principle of least privilege. There are various types of access control:

- Role-Based Access Control (RBAC): Access is granted based on users' roles or job functions. Users are assigned to predefined roles, and each role has specific permissions.
- Attribute-Based Access Control (ABAC): Access decisions are made based on attributes associated with users, resources, and environmental conditions.
- Discretionary Access Control (DAC): Owners of resources have control over who can access their resources and what level of access is granted.
- Mandatory Access Control (MAC): Access control policies are defined and enforced by the system, typically used in high-security environments.

1.8 Security Awareness and Training

Security awareness and training are critical components of a comprehensive cybersecurity strategy. They play a vital role in empowering employees and users to recognize and respond effectively to cybersecurity threats and risks. Here's why security awareness and training are essential:

1. Cybersecurity Education: Security awareness training educates employees and users about the various types of cyber threats, such as phishing, social engineering, and malware. It helps individuals understand the importance of cybersecurity and their role in protecting sensitive information.

2. Threat Recognition: By providing training on recognizing common cyber threats, users can identify suspicious emails, websites, or messages that could lead to security breaches.

3. Phishing Defense: Security awareness training can help users understand how to spot phishing attempts and avoid falling victim to deceptive tactics.

4. Password Security: Educating users about the importance of strong passwords, password hygiene, and the risks of password reuse helps enhance overall security.

5. Data Protection: Training users on data handling practices, data privacy, and the importance of securing sensitive information helps prevent data breaches.

6. Incident Reporting: Promoting a culture of reporting security incidents or suspicious activities allows for early detection and response to potential threats.

7. Safe Internet Usage: Educating users about safe browsing habits, the risks of downloading files from untrusted sources,

and the use of public Wi-Fi helps mitigate
cybersecurity risks.

8. Compliance: Security awareness training
helps organizations meet regulatory
requirements related to cybersecurity
awareness and employee training.

9. Insider Threat Mitigation: By raising
awareness about insider threats and
potential risks associated with internal
actors, organizations can mitigate the risk of
insider attacks.

10. Cybersecurity Best Practices: Training
sessions provide guidance on cybersecurity
best practices, helping users adopt safe
behaviors and avoid common pitfalls.

Module 2: Network Security

2.1 Network Architecture and Design

Network architecture and design refer to the planning and implementation of the structure and layout of a computer network. It involves making strategic decisions about how various network components will be interconnected to ensure efficient communication, data exchange, and secure operations. Here are key considerations in network architecture and design:

1. Requirements Gathering: Understand the organization's needs, objectives, and anticipated growth to determine the network's scope and capacity requirements.

2. Topology: Choose an appropriate network topology (e.g., star, bus, ring, mesh) that best suits the organization's needs and optimizes network performance and resilience.

3. Network Segmentation: Divide the network into smaller segments or subnetworks using techniques such as VLANs (Virtual Local Area Networks) to improve security, manage traffic, and isolate potential issues.

4. Network Devices: Select the right network devices, such as routers, switches, firewalls, and load balancers, to build a robust and scalable network infrastructure.

5. IP Addressing and Subnetting: Plan the allocation of IP addresses and subnetting schemes to efficiently manage network addressing and avoid IP conflicts.

6. Redundancy and High Availability: Implement redundancy and failover mechanisms to ensure network reliability and availability in case of device failures.

7. Security Measures: Incorporate security features, such as firewalls, intrusion detection systems, and encryption, to protect the network against cyber threats.

8. Bandwidth Management: Consider the bandwidth requirements of different network services and applications to prevent congestion and optimize network performance.

9. QoS (Quality of Service): Prioritize network traffic based on the importance of different

applications or services to ensure smooth operations and avoid bottlenecks.

10. Scalability: Design the network with scalability in mind, allowing for future growth and the addition of new devices and services without major disruptions.

11. Network Monitoring and Management: Implement network monitoring tools to proactively identify and address performance issues and security threats.

12. Cloud Integration: Consider how the network will connect to cloud services and plan for secure and efficient cloud integration.

13. Disaster Recovery and Business Continuity: Develop a disaster recovery plan and business continuity strategies to ensure network functionality during adverse events.

14. Compliance and Regulatory Requirements: Ensure that the network architecture complies with relevant industry standards and regulatory requirements.

15. Documentation: Maintain detailed documentation of the network design, configurations, and any changes made for ease of management and troubleshooting.

2.2 Firewalls and Intrusion Detection Systems (IDS)

Firewalls and Intrusion Detection Systems (IDS) are essential components of network security. They work together to protect networks and systems from cyber threats and unauthorized access. Here's an overview of each:

1. Firewalls:

- A firewall is a network security device or software that monitors and controls incoming and outgoing network traffic based on predefined rules.
- It acts as a barrier between a trusted internal network and an untrusted external network (typically the internet).
- Firewalls can be implemented at different points within the network, such as at the network perimeter (external firewall) or between internal segments (internal firewall).
- Types of firewalls include:
  - Stateful Inspection Firewall: Monitors the state of active connections and permits only legitimate traffic.
  - Proxy Firewall: Acts as an intermediary between internal and external network traffic, concealing internal addresses.
  - Next-Generation Firewall (NGFW): Combines traditional firewall capabilities with additional advanced features like application awareness and intrusion prevention.

- Firewalls help prevent unauthorized access, filter malicious traffic, and protect against common cyber threats like denial-of-service (DoS) attacks and port scanning.

2. Intrusion Detection Systems (IDS):
- IDS is a security system that monitors network or system activity for signs of suspicious behavior or potential security breaches.
- It analyzes network packets, log files, and other data sources to identify patterns and signatures associated with known cyber threats.
- IDS can be deployed as:
  - Network-Based IDS (NIDS): Monitors network traffic, usually at strategic points within the network.
  - Host-Based IDS (HIDS): Monitors activity on individual hosts or endpoints, such as servers and workstations.
- IDS can operate in two modes:
  - Signature-based: Matches patterns against a database of known attack signatures.

- Anomaly-based: Establishes a baseline of normal network behavior and detects deviations that may indicate attacks.
- When IDS detects suspicious activity or potential security breaches, it generates alerts to notify network administrators or security teams for investigation and response.

Firewalls and IDS work together to provide layered security for networks and systems. Firewalls act as a first line of defense, filtering and blocking incoming and outgoing traffic based on predefined rules. IDS complements this by monitoring network activity for signs of potential threats that may bypass the firewall's rules. When IDS detects abnormal behavior, it can trigger the firewall to take action, such as blocking the offending IP address or traffic.

By deploying firewalls and IDS, organizations can significantly enhance their network security, detect and respond to potential threats promptly, and safeguard their valuable data and assets from cyber-attacks.

2.3 Virtual Private Networks (VPNs) and Secure Socket Layer (SSL)

Virtual Private Networks (VPNs) and Secure Socket Layer (SSL) are both technologies used to enhance the security and privacy of data transmission over networks. However, they serve different purposes and operate at different layers of the network stack. Let's explore each in detail:

1. Virtual Private Network (VPN):
- A VPN is a technology that creates a secure and encrypted connection (tunnel) over a public or untrusted network, such as the internet.

- It allows users to securely access a private network remotely as if they were directly connected to it, even from outside the organization's physical premises.
- VPNs are commonly used to provide remote access for employees or enable secure communication between geographically distributed offices.
- The encrypted tunnel established by the VPN ensures that data transmitted between the user and the private network remains confidential and protected from potential eavesdropping or interception.
- There are different types of VPNs, such as site-to-site VPNs for connecting multiple sites, and remote access VPNs for individual users.

2. Secure Socket Layer (SSL) / Transport Layer Security (TLS):
- SSL is a deprecated predecessor of TLS, but the term SSL is still commonly used to refer to both SSL and TLS.

- SSL/TLS is a cryptographic protocol that operates at the transport layer of the network stack (Layer 4). It provides secure communication between clients and servers over a network.
- SSL/TLS is commonly used to secure web browsing. When you see "https://" in a website's URL, it indicates that the connection to that website is encrypted using SSL/TLS.
- SSL/TLS uses a combination of asymmetric (public-key) and symmetric encryption to secure data during transmission. It ensures data integrity, confidentiality, and authentication between the client and server.
- SSL/TLS certificates are used to verify the identity of the server, assuring users that they are connecting to the correct website.

In summary, VPNs are used to create secure and encrypted connections over public networks, allowing remote users to access a private network securely. SSL/TLS, on the other hand, is a cryptographic protocol used primarily for securing web communications and enabling encrypted communication between web browsers and servers. VPNs and SSL/TLS can be used together to provide comprehensive security for data transmission, particularly when accessing sensitive information over the internet.

2.4 Wireless Network Security

Wireless network security is crucial for protecting data and preventing unauthorized access in wireless communication environments. As wireless networks transmit data through radio signals, they are more susceptible to various security threats than wired networks. Here are some key considerations and best practices to enhance wireless network security:

1. Encryption: Enable strong encryption protocols, such as WPA2 (Wi-Fi Protected

Access 2) or WPA3, to protect data in transit between wireless devices and the access point. Avoid using older and less secure encryption methods like WEP (Wired Equivalent Privacy).

2. Secure Authentication: Use strong and unique passwords for the wireless network's pre-shared key (PSK) or employ enterprise-grade authentication methods, such as 802.1X with EAP (Extensible Authentication Protocol), for more robust and individualized user authentication.

3. SSID Broadcasting: Disable the broadcasting of the network's SSID (Service Set Identifier) to prevent the network from being easily discoverable by unauthorized users.

4. Network Segmentation: Implement network segmentation using VLANs (Virtual Local Area Networks) to isolate and

segregate different user groups, reducing the potential impact of security breaches.

5. Guest Network: Create a separate guest network to provide internet access for visitors and guests while keeping them isolated from internal resources.

6. Access Point Placement: Position wireless access points strategically to limit the network's coverage area and prevent unauthorized access from nearby locations.

7. MAC Address Filtering: Use MAC address filtering to allow only specific devices with pre-approved MAC addresses to connect to the wireless network.

8. Regular Firmware Updates: Keep the access points' firmware up to date with the latest security patches and updates to address known vulnerabilities.

9. Rogue Access Point Detection: Deploy tools to detect and prevent rogue access points that could potentially create security vulnerabilities within the network.

10. Wireless Intrusion Detection Systems (WIDS): Implement WIDS to monitor the wireless network for suspicious activities and unauthorized access attempts.

11. Physical Security: Ensure physical security for wireless access points to prevent tampering or unauthorized access.

12. Guest Network Isolation: Separate the guest network from the internal network to prevent unauthorized access to sensitive information.

13. Limit Signal Range: Adjust the power output of access points to limit the network's signal range and reduce the risk of unauthorized connections from a distance.

14. User Education: Educate users about wireless security best practices, such as not connecting to public Wi-Fi networks without VPN protection.

15. Continuous Monitoring: Regularly monitor and analyze network traffic to detect and respond to potential security incidents or anomalies.

By implementing these security measures, organizations can significantly enhance the security of their wireless networks, protect sensitive data, and ensure that only authorized users can access the network and its resources.

2.5 Network Monitoring and Incident Response

Network monitoring and incident response are crucial components of an effective cybersecurity strategy. They play a vital role in proactively identifying and responding to security incidents, ensuring the safety and integrity of the network. Here's an overview of network monitoring and incident response:

Network Monitoring:
1. Real-time Monitoring: Continuously monitor network traffic, system logs, and security events in real-time to detect anomalies, suspicious activities, or potential security breaches.

2. Network Traffic Analysis: Analyze network traffic patterns to identify unusual behavior or patterns that may indicate malicious activities, such as large data transfers or unusual access attempts.

3. Intrusion Detection Systems (IDS): Deploy IDS solutions to monitor network traffic and identify potential security threats and attacks, such as intrusion attempts or suspicious activities.

4. Log Analysis: Regularly review system logs, event logs, and security logs to identify signs of unauthorized access, malware infections, or other security incidents.

5. Security Information and Event Management (SIEM): Use SIEM tools to aggregate, correlate, and analyze security event data from various sources to provide a comprehensive view of the network's security posture.

6. Vulnerability Scanning: Perform regular vulnerability scans to identify potential weaknesses in the network and address them before they can be exploited by attackers.

Incident Response:
1. Incident Identification: Quickly identify and classify security incidents based on their severity and potential impact on the organization's assets and data.

2. Incident Containment: Isolate affected systems and networks to prevent the spread of the incident and minimize its impact on other parts of the network.

3. Incident Eradication: Take steps to eliminate the root cause of the incident and ensure that all traces of the threat actor's presence are removed from the network.

4. Incident Recovery: Restore affected systems and data to their normal state and ensure that business operations can resume as soon as possible.

5. Evidence Collection: Preserve and collect evidence related to the incident for further investigation and potential legal or law enforcement actions.

6. Post-Incident Analysis: Conduct a thorough post-mortem analysis of the incident to understand how it occurred,

identify lessons learned, and improve security measures to prevent similar incidents in the future.

7. Incident Reporting: Comply with relevant regulations and policies by reporting significant security incidents to appropriate internal and external stakeholders, such as management, customers, or regulatory authorities.

Network monitoring and incident response go hand in hand to protect the network from cyber threats. By implementing robust monitoring solutions and having a well-defined incident response plan in place, organizations can detect and respond to security incidents in a timely and effective manner, minimizing the potential impact and protecting sensitive data and resources.

Module 3: Operating System Security

3.1 Securing Operating Systems (Windows, macOS, Linux)

Securing operating systems (Windows, macOS, Linux) is crucial to protect computers and devices from cyber threats and ensure the confidentiality, integrity, and availability of data. Here are some essential security practices for each operating system:

1. Windows:
- Enable Windows Update: Regularly update the operating system and other software to

patch security vulnerabilities and improve system security.

- User Accounts: Use strong passwords for user accounts and consider implementing multi-factor authentication for added security.

- Firewall: Activate the built-in Windows Firewall or consider using third-party firewalls to monitor and control network traffic.

- Antivirus Software: Install reputable antivirus software and keep it up to date to detect and remove malware.

- User Access Control (UAC): Enable UAC to prompt for administrator approval before making significant system changes, preventing unauthorized modifications.

- Disable Unused Services: Disable or remove unnecessary services to reduce the attack surface.

2. macOS:
- Software Updates: Keep the macOS and applications up to date with the latest security patches.

- Gatekeeper: Use Gatekeeper to control the installation of apps from identified developers or the App Store, reducing the risk of installing malicious software.

- FileVault: Encrypt the startup disk with FileVault to protect data in case of theft or unauthorized access.

- Firewall: Enable the built-in macOS firewall or consider using third-party firewalls for network protection.

- Privacy Settings: Review and adjust privacy settings to restrict unnecessary access to system resources by applications.

3. Linux:
- Package Management: Use the package manager to keep Linux and installed software up to date, ensuring security patches are applied.

- Limited Privileges: Avoid using the root account for regular tasks; instead, use a standard user account with limited privileges.

- Firewall: Configure a firewall (e.g., iptables, firewalld) to control incoming and outgoing network traffic.

- Secure SSH: Securely configure SSH (Secure Shell) access, using key-based authentication and disabling root login.

- Disable Unneeded Services: Disable unnecessary services and daemons to reduce the attack surface.

- SELinux/AppArmor: Consider using SELinux or AppArmor to implement mandatory access controls and restrict access to resources.

General Security Practices for All Operating Systems:
- Backup Regularly: Perform regular backups of critical data to mitigate the impact of data loss due to malware or system failures.

- Strong Passwords: Use strong, unique passwords for all user accounts and consider using password managers to handle them securely.

- User Education: Educate users about phishing attacks, social engineering, and other common security threats to promote a security-aware culture.

- Application Whitelisting: Consider implementing application whitelisting to allow only approved applications to run on the system.

3.2 Patch Management and Software Updates

Patch management and software updates are crucial aspects of cybersecurity, as they help ensure that computer systems and software remain secure and protected against known vulnerabilities and exploits. Here's why patch management and software updates are essential and some best practices to follow:

Importance of Patch Management and Software Updates:

1. Security Vulnerabilities: Software vulnerabilities are regularly discovered, and

these weaknesses can be exploited by cybercriminals to gain unauthorized access, compromise data, or cause other security breaches.

2. Malware Protection: Software updates often include security patches that protect against newly identified malware and viruses, improving the system's overall resilience.

3. Data Protection: Keeping software up to date helps prevent data breaches and protects sensitive information from falling into the wrong hands.

4. System Stability: Updates not only fix security issues but also address bugs and performance issues, ensuring the system runs smoothly and efficiently.

5. Regulatory Compliance: Many industry regulations and data protection laws require

organizations to keep their systems and software updated to maintain compliance.

Best Practices for Patch Management and Software Updates:

1. Regular Updates: Establish a schedule to regularly check for and install updates for the operating system, applications, and security software.

2. Automated Updates: Enable automatic updates whenever possible to ensure critical security patches are promptly applied.

3. Test Updates: Before deploying updates across an entire organization, test them in a controlled environment to ensure they don't cause compatibility issues.

4. Prioritize Critical Updates: Prioritize security updates that address critical vulnerabilities to mitigate the highest risks first.

5. Keep Firmware Updated: Don't forget to update the firmware of hardware devices, such as routers and printers, to address security flaws.

6. Monitor Vendor Announcements: Stay informed about software vulnerabilities by subscribing to vendor security advisories and announcements.

7. Patch Third-Party Software: Ensure that third-party applications, plugins, and extensions are also kept up to date, as they can be potential entry points for attackers.

8. Centralized Management: Consider using patch management tools to centrally manage and deploy updates across the organization.

9. Backup Data: Before applying updates, perform regular data backups to protect against any unforeseen issues during the update process.

10. Maintain Inventory: Keep an up-to-date inventory of hardware and software assets to facilitate patch management and updates.

11. End-of-Life Software: Identify and retire end-of-life software that is no longer supported by vendors, as these applications are vulnerable to known exploits.

3.3 Host-based Intrusion Detection and Prevention

Host-based Intrusion Detection and Prevention Systems (HIDS/HIPS) are cybersecurity solutions designed to monitor and protect individual hosts or endpoints, such as servers, workstations, and other devices. Unlike network-based IDS/IPS that monitor network traffic, HIDS/HIPS focus on activities and events that occur on the host itself. Here's an overview of host-based intrusion detection and prevention:

Host-Based Intrusion Detection System (HIDS):

1. Monitoring Capabilities: HIDS continuously monitors the activity on a host, analyzing log files, system calls, file integrity, registry changes, and other host-specific events.

2. Anomaly Detection: HIDS looks for patterns or behaviors that deviate from normal activities, indicating potential security breaches or suspicious activities.

3. Signature-Based Detection: HIDS uses a database of known attack signatures to identify specific patterns associated with known malware and intrusion attempts.

4. Real-time Alerts: When HIDS detects suspicious activities or potential security incidents, it generates real-time alerts, notifying system administrators or security teams for further investigation.

5. File Integrity Monitoring (FIM): FIM checks the integrity of critical system files and directories to detect unauthorized modifications or tampering.

Host-Based Intrusion Prevention System (HIPS):

1. Proactive Blocking: HIPS can take immediate action to block or prevent suspicious or malicious activities on the host, such as terminating processes, blocking network connections, or quarantining files.

2. Policy Enforcement: HIPS enforces security policies on the host, ensuring that certain activities or applications comply with the organization's security guidelines.

3. Granular Controls: HIPS offers granular controls to define rules and policies based on specific behaviors or events, allowing

organizations to customize their security responses.

Benefits of HIDS/HIPS:

1. Visibility: HIDS/HIPS provide detailed insights into the activities and behavior of individual hosts, enabling administrators to detect threats and investigate incidents effectively.

2. Protection Against Zero-Day Attacks: HIDS/HIPS can detect and prevent unknown or zero-day attacks by analyzing behavior rather than relying solely on known attack signatures.

3. Early Threat Detection: HIDS/HIPS can detect threats early in the kill chain, minimizing the potential damage caused by security breaches.

4. Host-Centric Defense: HIDS/HIPS focus on protecting the individual host,

complementing network-based security solutions and providing an additional layer of defense.

5. Incident Response: HIDS/HIPS data can be valuable in incident response investigations, providing crucial information about the attack's origin and impact.

Limitations of HIDS/HIPS:

1. Resource Consumption: HIDS/HIPS can consume significant system resources, potentially impacting host performance.

2. Localized Protection: HIDS/HIPS protect individual hosts but may not detect network-level threats or attacks that do not directly target the host.

To maximize the effectiveness of host-based intrusion detection and prevention, organizations should integrate HIDS/HIPS into their broader cybersecurity strategy, combining them with network-based security measures, user education, and proactive vulnerability management.

3.4 Securing Mobile Devices

Securing mobile devices is essential as they store and access a significant amount of sensitive data and are vulnerable to various security threats. Here are some best practices to enhance the security of mobile devices:

1. Device Lock and Biometrics: Set up a strong device lock (e.g., PIN, password, pattern) and enable biometric authentication (fingerprint or facial recognition) to prevent unauthorized access.

2. Encryption: Enable device encryption to protect data stored on the device in case it falls into the wrong hands.

3. Regular Updates: Keep the device's operating system, apps, and firmware up to date with the latest security patches and updates.

4. App Source: Download apps only from official app stores (e.g., Google Play Store, Apple App Store) to minimize the risk of downloading malicious apps.

5. App Permissions: Review app permissions before installation and grant only necessary permissions to apps.

6. App Whitelisting: Consider using app whitelisting to allow only approved apps to run on the device.

7. Mobile Device Management (MDM): Use MDM solutions to manage and enforce security policies on corporate-owned devices.

8. Remote Wipe and Lock: Enable remote wipe and lock features to erase data and lock the device remotely in case of loss or theft.

9. Secure Wi-Fi: Avoid connecting to public Wi-Fi networks without a VPN (Virtual Private Network) to encrypt data transmission.

10. Mobile Antivirus: Install reputable mobile security solutions that include antivirus and anti-malware features.

11. Mobile VPN: Use a mobile VPN to secure internet connections and protect data when using public Wi-Fi.

12. Two-Factor Authentication (2FA): Enable two-factor authentication for online accounts to add an extra layer of security.

13. Avoid Jailbreaking or Rooting: Avoid jailbreaking (iOS) or rooting (Android) the device, as it exposes it to more security risks.

14. Secure Data Backup: Regularly back up data to a secure cloud service or a trusted local storage solution.

15. User Education: Educate users about mobile security best practices, such as avoiding clicking on suspicious links or phishing emails.

By following these mobile device security best practices, users can significantly reduce the risk of data breaches, malware infections, and other security incidents, ensuring the confidentiality and integrity of their sensitive information.

Module 4: Application Security

4.1 Web Application Security

Web application security is essential to protect web-based applications from various security threats and vulnerabilities. Web applications are exposed to potential attacks, making them a prime target for cybercriminals. Here are some best practices and strategies to enhance web application security:

1. Input Validation: Implement robust input validation mechanisms to prevent common attacks like SQL injection, Cross-Site Scripting (XSS), and Cross-Site Request Forgery (CSRF). Validate and sanitize all user input before processing it.

2. Secure Coding Practices: Follow secure coding practices, such as avoiding hardcoded credentials, using parameterized queries,

and escaping output to prevent injection attacks.

3. Authentication and Authorization: Enforce strong authentication mechanisms, including multi-factor authentication (MFA), and implement granular authorization to ensure users have access only to the necessary resources.

4. Session Management: Use secure session management techniques, such as unique session IDs, session timeouts, and secure cookie settings.

5. HTTPS Encryption: Enable HTTPS (TLS/SSL) for all communication between clients and the web server to encrypt data in transit and prevent man-in-the-middle attacks.

6. Error Handling: Implement proper error handling to avoid exposing sensitive information to attackers and users.

7. Security Headers: Utilize security headers (e.g., Content Security Policy, HTTP Strict Transport Security) to provide additional layers of protection against various attacks.

8. Regular Security Testing: Conduct regular security assessments, including penetration testing and vulnerability scanning, to identify and fix potential security flaws.

9. Secure File Uploads: Validate file types and extensions for uploaded files and store them in a secure location outside the web root.

10. Least Privilege: Follow the principle of least privilege and grant the minimum required permissions to web application components and database accounts.

11. Web Application Firewall (WAF): Consider deploying a WAF to filter and block malicious traffic, offering an additional layer of protection.

12. Software Updates: Keep web application frameworks, libraries, and third-party components up to date with the latest security patches.

13. User Education: Educate users about potential web application security risks, such as phishing attacks and the importance of using strong passwords.

14. Secure Development Lifecycle: Incorporate security throughout the entire software development lifecycle, from design to deployment.

15. Monitor and Respond: Implement logging and monitoring to detect and respond to potential security incidents promptly.

By adopting these web application security practices, organizations can reduce the risk of security breaches, protect sensitive data, and ensure the reliability and trustworthiness of their web applications.

4.2 Secure Coding Practices

Secure coding practices are essential for developing software that is resistant to security vulnerabilities and less susceptible to cyber-attacks. Writing secure code from the outset helps prevent potential security flaws and ensures the confidentiality, integrity, and availability of the application and its data. Here are some key secure coding practices to follow:

1. Input Validation: Always validate and sanitize all user input to prevent injection attacks (e.g., SQL injection, XSS). Use parameterized queries for database access.

2. Output Encoding: Encode output data to prevent XSS attacks. Use appropriate encoding functions when displaying user-generated content on web pages.

3. Avoid Hardcoded Credentials: Never hardcode sensitive information, such as passwords or API keys, directly into the code. Store credentials securely in configuration files or use environment variables.

4. Avoid Insecure APIs: Use secure APIs and libraries with proper authentication and authorization mechanisms. Be cautious when using third-party libraries and ensure they are from trusted sources.

5. Secure Session Management: Implement secure session management techniques, such as using secure session IDs, setting proper session timeouts, and enabling secure cookie settings.

6. Error Handling: Implement proper error handling to avoid exposing sensitive information to potential attackers.

7. Secure File Handling: Validate file types and extensions for uploaded files, store them in secure locations, and avoid executing uploaded files.

8. Least Privilege Principle: Grant the minimum necessary permissions to users, processes, and applications to reduce the potential impact of security breaches.

9. HTTPS Encryption: Use HTTPS (TLS/SSL) for all communication between clients and servers to encrypt data in transit and prevent man-in-the-middle attacks.

10. Security Headers: Utilize security headers (e.g., Content Security Policy, HTTP Strict Transport Security) to provide additional layers of protection against various attacks.

11. Avoid Buffer Overflows: Use safe string manipulation functions to prevent buffer overflows and potential memory corruption.

12. Regular Updates: Keep software dependencies and components up to date with the latest security patches.

13. Secure Configuration: Ensure that server configurations, permissions, and access controls are set securely to prevent unauthorized access.

14. Input Length Validation: Validate the length of input data to prevent buffer overflow and denial-of-service attacks.

15. Review Code: Conduct thorough code reviews and security assessments to identify and fix potential security flaws.

4.3 Input Validation and Output Encoding

Input validation and output encoding are crucial secure coding practices used to prevent various types of web application vulnerabilities, especially Cross-Site Scripting

(XSS) attacks. Let's delve into each of these practices:

1. Input Validation:
Input validation involves verifying and sanitizing all user-supplied data before processing or displaying it. The goal is to ensure that the data adheres to the expected format and does not contain malicious or unexpected content. Proper input validation helps prevent common security issues such as SQL injection and XSS attacks.

Key principles of input validation:

- Validate on the Server: Perform input validation on the server-side, as client-side validation can be bypassed by attackers.

- Use Whitelisting: Accept only known valid characters and data patterns, known as whitelisting. Reject anything that does not match the expected format.

- Avoid Blacklisting: Avoid using blacklisting (blocking specific characters or patterns) as it may be less effective and prone to evasion.

- Sanitize Data: If validation fails, sanitize the data to remove any harmful or unwanted content. This step is particularly important for preventing XSS attacks.

- Validate All Inputs: Validate all user inputs, including form fields, URL parameters, cookies, and headers.

2. Output Encoding:
Output encoding involves encoding or escaping data before displaying it in a web application to ensure that the data is interpreted as data and not executable code. Proper output encoding is critical for preventing XSS attacks, where attackers inject malicious scripts into web pages.

Types of Output Encoding:

- HTML Encoding: Encode special characters in HTML, such as `<`, `>`, `&`, `"`, and `'`, into their respective HTML entities (e.g., `&lt;`, `&gt;`, `&amp;`, `&quot;`, `&#39;`).

- URL Encoding: Encode special characters in URLs using percent-encoding (e.g., space becomes `%20`, ampersand becomes `%26`).

- JavaScript Encoding: Encode data displayed within JavaScript contexts using functions like `encodeURIComponent()` or escaping special characters.

Benefits of Input Validation and Output Encoding:

1. Mitigating XSS Attacks: By validating input and encoding output, web applications can effectively prevent XSS attacks and protect users from malicious scripts.

2. Preventing Injection Attacks: Input validation helps prevent injection attacks,

such as SQL injection, by ensuring that data adheres to the expected format.

3. Improving Data Integrity: Proper input validation ensures that the data processed by the application is valid and reliable, leading to better data integrity.

4. Enhancing Application Security: By incorporating these practices into the development process, web applications become more robust and secure against common security vulnerabilities.

5. Protecting Users: Input validation and output encoding help protect users from potential threats and keep their sensitive information safe.

Overall, input validation and output encoding are essential security measures that developers should implement as part of their secure coding practices to safeguard web applications and ensure a safer online experience for users.

4.4 Security Testing and Code Review

Security testing and code review are two crucial activities in the software development lifecycle that help identify and address security vulnerabilities in applications. Both practices complement each other, providing different perspectives on security assurance. Let's explore each of them:

1. Security Testing:
Security testing is a systematic evaluation of a software application's security to identify potential weaknesses, vulnerabilities, and flaws that attackers could exploit. It involves various techniques and tools to assess the application's security posture and ensure that it meets security requirements.

Types of Security Testing:

- Penetration Testing: Simulates real-world attacks to identify vulnerabilities and weaknesses in the application.

- Vulnerability Scanning: Automated tools scan the application for known vulnerabilities.

- Security Code Review: Manual or automated examination of the application's source code to find security issues.

- Security Configuration Review: Assessing the security configuration of servers, databases, and network devices.

- Authentication and Authorization Testing: Evaluating the effectiveness of authentication and authorization mechanisms.

- Data Security Testing: Assessing data protection mechanisms, including encryption and data access controls.

2. Code Review:

Code review involves a thorough examination of the application's source code by experienced developers or security experts. The primary goal is to identify coding flaws, security vulnerabilities, and potential weaknesses in the codebase. Code reviews ensure that the code adheres to secure coding practices, industry standards, and the organization's security policies.

Benefits of Security Testing and Code Review:

1. Early Vulnerability Detection: Both practices identify security issues early in the development process, reducing the cost of fixing them at later stages.

2. Comprehensive Assessment: Security testing provides a holistic view of the application's security, while code review focuses on code-level vulnerabilities.

3. Continuous Improvement: Regular security testing and code reviews promote a culture of continuous improvement and security awareness within the development team.

4. Compliance and Risk Mitigation: Identifying and fixing security vulnerabilities helps meet compliance requirements and reduces the risk of potential security breaches.

5. Enhanced Application Security: Combining security testing and code review leads to stronger and more secure applications that are resilient to cyber-attacks.

6. Developer Education: Code reviews serve as a knowledge-sharing platform, enabling

less-experienced developers to learn from more experienced team members.

It's important to integrate security testing and code review into the development process and conduct them throughout the software development lifecycle. By doing so, organizations can deliver more secure applications, protect sensitive data, and maintain a strong security posture against evolving threats.

4.5 Application Security Tools

Application security tools are software solutions designed to assist developers and security teams in identifying, assessing, and mitigating security vulnerabilities in applications. These tools automate various security testing processes and provide insights into potential weaknesses, helping to improve the overall security posture of software applications. Here are some common types of application security tools:

1. Static Application Security Testing (SAST) Tools:

SAST tools analyze the source code or application's binary without executing it. They identify security vulnerabilities, coding flaws, and potential weaknesses in the codebase. SAST tools help developers catch security issues early in the development process.

2. Dynamic Application Security Testing (DAST) Tools:

DAST tools evaluate web applications from the outside-in by simulating real-world attacks. They test applications in running environments to identify vulnerabilities like SQL injection, XSS, and insecure authentication.

3. Interactive Application Security Testing (IAST) Tools:

IAST tools combine aspects of SAST and DAST. They analyze the application's code while it's running, providing real-time security testing insights during development and testing.

4. Software Composition Analysis (SCA) Tools:
SCA tools examine third-party libraries and components used in the application to identify known vulnerabilities and license compliance issues. They help manage open-source dependencies securely.

5. Web Application Firewalls (WAF):
WAFs are security appliances or cloud-based services that protect web applications from malicious traffic and various types of web attacks, including SQL injection and XSS.

6. Runtime Application Self-Protection (RASP) Tools:
RASP tools are designed to protect applications at runtime by monitoring

application behavior and preventing malicious activities.

7. Vulnerability Scanners:
Vulnerability scanners automatically scan applications to detect security flaws, misconfigurations, and outdated components.

8. Penetration Testing Tools:
Penetration testing tools, also known as ethical hacking tools, simulate real attacks on applications to identify vulnerabilities and assess their impact on security.

9. Secure Code Review Tools:
Secure code review tools automate the process of reviewing application code for security issues, ensuring adherence to secure coding practices.

10. Mobile Application Security Testing (MAST) Tools:

MAST tools focus on mobile app security, identifying vulnerabilities unique to mobile platforms.

11. Cloud Security Tools:
Cloud security tools assess the security of applications deployed in cloud environments, ensuring that best practices are followed.

12. Container Security Tools:
Container security tools analyze and secure containerized applications, ensuring the security of Docker and Kubernetes environments.

Module 6: Cryptography

6.1 Introduction to Cryptography

Cryptography is the science and practice of secure communication in the presence of adversaries. It is an ancient art that involves transforming plaintext (readable data) into ciphertext (encoded data) to protect sensitive information from unauthorized access. Cryptography plays a crucial role in ensuring confidentiality, integrity, and authenticity of data in various fields, including online communication, financial transactions, and data storage.

Applications of Cryptography:

1. Secure Communication: Cryptography ensures secure communication over the internet, protecting data during transmission.

2. Data Privacy: Cryptography safeguards sensitive data in storage, databases, and cloud environments.

3. Secure Transactions: Cryptography secures financial transactions, online purchases, and electronic banking.

4. Digital Certificates: Cryptography enables the issuance and verification of digital certificates, such as SSL/TLS certificates for secure websites.

5. Password Security: Cryptographic hashing protects user passwords in databases, preventing plain-text storage.

Cryptography is a fundamental tool for modern-day cybersecurity, playing a crucial role in protecting sensitive information and ensuring secure digital communication across various industries and applications.

6.2 Symmetric and Asymmetric Encryption

Symmetric encryption and asymmetric encryption are two fundamental cryptographic techniques used to secure data and enable secure communication between parties. They differ in how encryption and decryption keys are used and shared. Let's explore the characteristics of each:

1. Symmetric Encryption:

- Also known as Secret-Key Cryptography or Conventional Cryptography.
- Uses the same secret key for both encryption and decryption processes.
- The sender and the receiver must possess and keep the secret key secret to ensure secure communication.
- Fast and efficient for encrypting and decrypting large amounts of data.
- Key distribution is a challenge since the same key needs to be securely shared between parties.
- Well-suited for scenarios where speed and efficiency are critical and a secure channel for key exchange is available.

- Examples of symmetric encryption algorithms include AES (Advanced Encryption Standard) and DES (Data Encryption Standard).

2. Asymmetric Encryption:

- Also known as Public-Key Cryptography.
- Uses a pair of mathematically related keys: a public key and a private key.
- The public key is used for encryption, and the private key is used for decryption.
- The public key can be freely distributed and shared with anyone, while the private key must be kept secret and only known to the owner.
- Provides secure key exchange and authentication, as it allows one party to send encrypted data that only the intended recipient can decrypt using their private key.
- Slower and more resource-intensive than symmetric encryption, making it less efficient for encrypting large amounts of data.

- Examples of asymmetric encryption algorithms include RSA (Rivest-Shamir-Adleman) and ECC (Elliptic Curve Cryptography).

Comparison:

- Symmetric encryption is faster and more efficient for bulk data encryption, while asymmetric encryption is used for secure key exchange and digital signatures.
- Symmetric encryption requires a secure method to share the secret key between parties, whereas asymmetric encryption allows for secure communication without requiring a pre-shared secret key.
- Asymmetric encryption provides more robust security for scenarios where key distribution and authentication are crucial.

In practice, both symmetric and asymmetric encryption are often used together to achieve a combination of efficiency and security. For instance, in SSL/TLS connections, asymmetric encryption is used to establish a secure connection and exchange a symmetric session key, which is then used for efficient symmetric encryption during the data transfer.

6.3 Public Key Infrastructure (PKI)

Public Key Infrastructure (PKI) is a comprehensive system of hardware, software, policies, and procedures used to manage and secure the generation, distribution, storage, and revocation of digital certificates. PKI enables secure communication and data exchange over the internet and other networks by facilitating the use of asymmetric encryption and digital signatures.

Key components of a PKI include:

1. Public and Private Keys: PKI uses asymmetric encryption, which involves a pair

of mathematically related keys – a public key and a private key. The public key is widely distributed and used for encryption and verifying digital signatures, while the private key is kept secret and used for decryption and creating digital signatures.

2. Digital Certificates: Digital certificates bind a public key to an identity (e.g., individual, organization, or website). They are issued by a trusted Certificate Authority (CA) and include the public key, identity information, and a digital signature from the CA to ensure its authenticity.

3. Certificate Authorities (CAs): CAs are trusted entities that issue digital certificates to individuals, organizations, or devices after verifying their identity. They play a critical role in validating the ownership of public keys and ensuring the integrity of the PKI.

4. Registration Authority (RA): The RA assists the CA in verifying the identity of certificate

applicants and managing certificate enrollment processes.

5. Certificate Revocation: PKI includes mechanisms to revoke certificates if they are compromised or no longer valid. Certificate revocation lists (CRLs) and Online Certificate Status Protocol (OCSP) are used to check the validity of certificates.

6. Certification Practice Statement (CPS): The CPS is a document that outlines the CA's policies and practices regarding certificate issuance, management, and revocation.

How PKI Works:

1. Certificate Generation: The process begins with generating a public-private key pair. The public key is included in a certificate signing

request (CSR) along with identity information.

2. Certificate Enrollment: The CSR is submitted to a CA for verification. The CA validates the identity of the applicant before issuing the digital certificate.

3. Certificate Distribution: Once the certificate is issued, it is distributed to the certificate holder, and the corresponding private key is securely stored by the owner.

4. Secure Communication: When parties want to communicate securely, they exchange and use each other's public keys to encrypt and decrypt messages and verify digital signatures.

5. Certificate Revocation: If a private key is compromised or the certificate is no longer valid, the certificate can be revoked, and the CRL or OCSP is used to check its status.

PKI is widely used in various applications, including SSL/TLS encryption for secure websites, email encryption, digital signatures, VPN authentication, and secure document signing. It provides a foundation for establishing trust, confidentiality, and data integrity in modern communication and e-commerce.

6.4 Digital Signatures and Certificates

Digital signatures and certificates are essential components of Public Key Infrastructure (PKI) and play a crucial role in ensuring the authenticity, integrity, and non-repudiation of digital data and communications. Let's explore each of these concepts:

1. Digital Signatures:

- A digital signature is a cryptographic technique that provides a way to verify the authenticity and integrity of digital documents, messages, or transactions.

- It involves using a private key to create a unique digital signature that is appended to the digital content.

- The digital signature can be verified using the corresponding public key, which ensures that the data has not been altered since the signature was applied and that it was signed by the holder of the private key.

- Digital signatures provide non-repudiation, meaning that the signer cannot deny having signed the document.

- The process of creating a digital signature involves hashing the digital content and encrypting the hash using the signer's private key.

- The recipient of the digitally signed content can verify the signature using the signer's public key and comparing the decrypted hash with a newly calculated hash of the received content.

2. Digital Certificates:

- A digital certificate is an electronic document that binds a public key to an entity's identity, such as an individual, organization, or website.
- It serves as a form of identification and enables secure communication and authentication in PKI environments.
- Digital certificates are issued by trusted Certificate Authorities (CAs) after verifying the identity of the certificate holder.
- A digital certificate contains the following information:
  - The public key of the certificate holder.
  - The identity information of the certificate holder (e.g., name, organization).
  - The digital signature of the CA, which ensures the certificate's authenticity and integrity.
  - The certificate's validity period (start and end dates).

- Digital certificates are used for various purposes, including SSL/TLS encryption for secure websites, email encryption and signing, VPN authentication, and code signing for software integrity.

How Digital Signatures and Certificates Work Together:

- To digitally sign a document or message, the sender generates a digital signature using their private key and appends it to the content.
- The recipient of the digitally signed content can use the sender's public key, obtained from their digital certificate, to verify the signature's authenticity and integrity.
- If the digital signature is valid, it confirms that the document or message was indeed signed by the sender, and the content has not been altered since the signature was applied.

Digital signatures and certificates are vital for secure online transactions, electronic document authentication, and establishing trust between parties. They are crucial components in building a secure and reliable digital communication infrastructure.

6.5 Cryptographic Attacks and Countermeasures

Cryptographic attacks are techniques used by adversaries to compromise the security of cryptographic systems and break encryption. These attacks aim to exploit weaknesses or vulnerabilities in cryptographic algorithms, protocols, or implementations. To defend against these attacks, countermeasures are employed to enhance the security of cryptographic systems. Let's explore some common cryptographic attacks and the countermeasures used to mitigate them:

1. Brute-Force Attack:

- In a brute-force attack, the attacker systematically tries all possible combinations of keys to decrypt encrypted data.
Countermeasure:
- Use strong encryption keys with sufficient length and complexity to make brute-forcing infeasible.
- Implement mechanisms to detect and block multiple failed authentication attempts.

2. Man-in-the-Middle (MITM) Attack:
- In an MITM attack, the attacker intercepts and alters communications between two parties, often without their knowledge.
Countermeasure:
- Use secure key exchange mechanisms, such as Diffie-Hellman, to prevent eavesdropping and MITM attacks.
- Implement digital certificates and digital signatures to verify the authenticity of communication endpoints.

3. Known Plaintext Attack:

- In a known plaintext attack, the attacker has access to pairs of plaintext and corresponding ciphertext, attempting to deduce the encryption key.
Countermeasure:
- Use secure encryption algorithms that are resistant to known plaintext attacks.
- Ensure the key used in encryption is not predictable or derived from easily accessible data.

4. Chosen Plaintext Attack:
- In a chosen plaintext attack, the attacker can select specific plaintext and observe the corresponding ciphertext to deduce the encryption key.
Countermeasure:
- Use encryption algorithms with strong security properties, such as resistance to chosen plaintext attacks.
- Implement secure padding mechanisms to prevent information leakage.

5. Birthday Attack:

- A birthday attack exploits the probability that, in a large set of data, two different inputs can produce the same hash value.
Countermeasure:
- Use cryptographic hash functions with sufficient bit length to reduce the likelihood of collisions in the hash output.

6. Differential Cryptanalysis:
- Differential cryptanalysis is an attack that analyzes the differences in plaintext inputs and their corresponding ciphertexts to deduce the encryption key.
Countermeasure:
- Implement encryption algorithms with strong resistance to differential cryptanalysis.
- Use multiple rounds of encryption to increase the complexity of the attack.

7. Side-Channel Attacks:
- Side-channel attacks exploit unintended information leaked by the cryptographic system, such as power consumption,

electromagnetic radiation, or timing variations.

Countermeasure:

- Implement countermeasures like constant-time algorithms and secure hardware to prevent side-channel attacks.

- Use hardware and software techniques to mask or eliminate side-channel information.

Module 7: Incident Response and Cyber Forensics

7.1 Incident Response Process and Best Practices

Incident response is a structured approach to managing and mitigating cybersecurity incidents promptly and effectively. It involves detecting, analyzing, containing, eradicating, and recovering from security breaches or cyber-attacks. Having a well-defined incident response plan and following best practices are crucial for minimizing the impact of security incidents. Here are some incident response best practices:

1. Develop an Incident Response Plan:
- Create a comprehensive incident response plan tailored to your organization's specific needs, outlining roles, responsibilities, communication channels, and escalation procedures.

2. Establish an Incident Response Team (IRT):
- Assemble a dedicated team comprising IT staff, security experts, legal personnel, and other relevant stakeholders to handle incidents efficiently.

3. Incident Identification and Detection:
- Implement robust monitoring and detection systems to identify potential security incidents promptly. This includes

intrusion detection systems, log analysis, and security event monitoring.

4. Classification and Prioritization:
- Classify and prioritize incidents based on their severity and potential impact to allocate resources effectively.

5. Containment and Mitigation:
- Quickly isolate and contain the affected systems to prevent further damage. Implement temporary fixes to mitigate the immediate impact of the incident.

6. Investigation and Analysis:
- Thoroughly investigate the incident to understand the attack vector, affected systems, and data compromised. Preserve evidence for potential legal or forensic investigations.

7. Communication and Reporting:
- Maintain clear communication within the incident response team and inform relevant

stakeholders, such as management, legal, and law enforcement (if necessary).

8. Data Breach Notifications:
- Comply with data breach notification laws and regulations by promptly notifying affected individuals and authorities, if required.

9. Eradication and Recovery:
- Remove the root cause of the incident and restore affected systems to their normal state. Ensure that all malware and unauthorized access points are eradicated.

10. Post-Incident Review (Post-Mortem):
- Conduct a post-incident review to analyze the response process, identify areas for improvement, and update the incident response plan accordingly.

11. Continuous Improvement:

- Continuously update and enhance incident response capabilities based on lessons learned from previous incidents and emerging threats.

12. Training and Awareness:
- Regularly train employees on incident response procedures and raise awareness about the importance of cybersecurity.

13. Cybersecurity Hygiene:
- Maintain good cybersecurity hygiene, such as regular patching, strong access controls, and network segmentation, to prevent common attack vectors.

14. Backup and Disaster Recovery:
- Regularly back up critical data and implement disaster recovery measures to facilitate quick recovery after an incident.

By following these best practices, organizations can effectively respond to security incidents, minimize the impact of breaches, and protect sensitive data and assets. Incident response is an ongoing process that requires collaboration, vigilance, and continuous improvement to stay ahead of evolving cybersecurity threats.

7.2 Cyber Forensics Techniques

Cyber forensic techniques are investigative methods used to collect, preserve, analyze, and present digital evidence related to cybersecurity incidents or criminal activities. These techniques help identify the root cause of cyber incidents, reconstruct events, and attribute actions to specific individuals or entities. Here are some common cyber forensic techniques:

1. Digital Evidence Collection:
- Identify and collect digital evidence from various sources, such as computers, mobile devices, servers, and network logs.

- Use forensically sound methods to ensure the integrity and admissibility of evidence in legal proceedings.

2. Disk Imaging:
- Create a bit-by-bit copy (disk image) of storage media to preserve the original data for analysis while keeping the evidence intact.

3. File Carving:
- Recover deleted or fragmented files from storage media by searching for file headers and footers.

4. Memory Forensics:
- Analyze volatile memory (RAM) to retrieve information like running processes, open network connections, and encryption keys.

5. Network Forensics:
- Analyze network traffic and logs to reconstruct communication patterns and identify malicious activities.

6. Malware Analysis:
- Analyze malware to understand its behavior, functionality, and potential impact on systems and networks.

7. Timeline Analysis:
- Construct a chronological timeline of events related to the incident to understand the sequence of activities.

8. Metadata Analysis:
- Examine metadata associated with files and documents to identify timestamps, authorship, and other relevant information.

9. Hashing and Digital Signatures:
- Use hashing and digital signatures to verify the integrity of digital evidence and ensure it has not been altered.

10. Steganography Detection:

- Identify hidden data or messages within images, audio files, or other media using steganography detection tools.

11. Email and Internet Forensics:
- Investigate email headers, attachments, and internet activities to trace communication and online activities.

12. Mobile Device Forensics:
- Extract data from mobile devices, including call logs, messages, application data, and location information.

13. Cloud Forensics:
- Investigate data stored in cloud environments and determine its relevance to the investigation.

14. Registry Analysis:
- Examine the Windows registry for artifacts that can provide insights into user activities and system changes.

15. Data Recovery:
- Attempt to recover data from damaged or corrupted storage media.

It is essential to conduct cyber forensic investigations following established procedures and legal guidelines to ensure the admissibility of evidence in court. Cyber forensic professionals should have expertise in data analysis, data recovery, programming, and legal procedures to effectively conduct investigations and support legal proceedings.

7.3 Preservation and Analysis of Digital Evidence

Preservation and analysis of digital evidence are critical steps in cyber forensic investigations to ensure the integrity, authenticity, and admissibility of evidence in legal proceedings. These steps involve careful handling, documentation, and analysis of digital data to reconstruct events and identify potential malicious activities. Here's a guide on preserving and analyzing digital evidence:

Preservation of Digital Evidence:

1. Documentation:
- Thoroughly document the initial state of the digital evidence, including the location, time of discovery, and the person who collected it.
- Maintain a chain of custody log to track the possession and movement of the evidence.

2. Secure Collection:
- Use forensically sound procedures to collect digital evidence to prevent alteration or contamination.
- Create a bit-by-bit copy (disk image) of storage media to preserve the original data.

3. Isolation:
- Isolate the affected systems or devices from the network to prevent further compromise and damage.
- Use write-blocking hardware or software tools to prevent accidental modifications during the collection process.

4. Physical Security:
- Store digital evidence in a secure physical location to protect it from unauthorized access, tampering, or theft.

5. Hashing:
- Generate cryptographic hashes (e.g., SHA-256) of the original evidence and the copied images to verify integrity throughout the investigation.

6. Redundant Backup:

- Create redundant backups of digital evidence to avoid data loss due to hardware failure or accidental deletions.

Analysis of Digital Evidence:

1. Forensic Imaging:
- Analyze the disk images using forensic tools to examine the entire data without modifying the original evidence.

2. Timeline Analysis:
- Create a chronological timeline of events to understand the sequence of activities leading to the incident.

3. File Carving:
- Recover deleted or partially overwritten files using file carving techniques to extract evidence from unallocated space.

4. Metadata Analysis:

- Examine metadata (e.g., timestamps, file properties) to determine the creation, modification, and access times of files.

5. Registry Analysis:
- Analyze the Windows registry to uncover user activities, software installations, and system changes.

6. Network Traffic Analysis:
- Investigate network logs and packet captures to identify communication patterns and suspicious activities.

7. Memory Forensics:
- Analyze volatile memory (RAM) to identify running processes, open network connections, and potential malware.

8. Keyword Search:

- Use keyword searches to locate relevant files, messages, or other digital artifacts related to the investigation.

9. Cryptanalysis:
- Attempt to decrypt encrypted files or communications if encryption keys are available.

10. Malware Analysis:
- Investigate malware behavior and functionality to understand its impact on systems and networks.

11. Reconstruction of Events:
- Use the analysis results to reconstruct the incident's timeline and provide a clear picture of what occurred.

12. Reporting:

- Document all findings, methods, and results in a comprehensive forensic report suitable for presentation in legal proceedings.

7.4 Legal and Ethical Considerations in Cyber Forensics

In cyber forensics, there are several legal and ethical considerations that investigators must adhere to while handling digital evidence and conducting investigations. These considerations help ensure that investigations are conducted lawfully, ethically, and in compliance with applicable regulations. Here are some key legal and ethical considerations in cyber forensics:

1. Legal Authorization:
- Obtain proper legal authorization before conducting any cyber forensic investigation. This may involve obtaining search warrants or other legal orders, depending on the

jurisdiction and the nature of the investigation.

2. Chain of Custody:
- Maintain a strict chain of custody for all digital evidence collected during the investigation. Document each transfer or handling of the evidence to preserve its integrity and admissibility in court.

3. Privacy Rights:
- Respect individuals' privacy rights during the investigation. Avoid accessing or examining data that is not directly relevant to the investigation.

4. Data Privacy Laws:
- Comply with data privacy laws and regulations that govern the collection, storage, and use of personal data during cyber forensic investigations.

5. Admissibility of Evidence:
- Ensure that all evidence collected follows the rules of evidence and is admissible in court. This includes using forensically sound methods and tools to collect and analyze digital evidence.

6. Expertise and Qualifications:
- Cyber forensic investigators should have the necessary expertise, qualifications, and training to conduct investigations competently and professionally.

7. Scope of Investigation:
- Limit the scope of the investigation to the authorized purpose and avoid unnecessarily intruding into areas beyond the investigation's scope.

8. Confidentiality:
- Maintain confidentiality and protect sensitive information obtained during the

investigation to prevent unauthorized disclosure.

9. Cross-Border Considerations:
- Be aware of cross-border legal issues when conducting international cyber forensic investigations, as laws and regulations may vary significantly between jurisdictions.

10. Avoid Destruction of Evidence:
- Take precautions to prevent accidental destruction or alteration of digital evidence during the investigation.

11. Collaboration with Law Enforcement:
- Work closely and collaboratively with law enforcement agencies when necessary, ensuring that information sharing follows proper legal channels.

12. Ethical Conduct:
- Uphold ethical standards throughout the investigation process, treating all parties involved with respect and fairness.

13. Transparency:
- Be transparent about the investigative process and findings, providing clear and accurate reporting to all relevant parties.

14. Informed Consent:
- Obtain informed consent from individuals or organizations involved in the investigation, where applicable and legally required.

Module 8: Ethical Hacking and Penetration Testing

8.1 Introduction to Ethical Hacking

Ethical hacking, also known as penetration testing or white-hat hacking, is a cybersecurity practice where authorized professionals, known as ethical hackers, simulate cyber-attacks on computer systems, networks, applications, and other digital assets to identify and fix security vulnerabilities. The primary goal of ethical hacking is to proactively assess an organization's security posture and help improve its overall cybersecurity defenses. Ethical hacking is conducted with the explicit permission and consent of the organization or entity being tested. Here's an introduction to ethical hacking:

1. Purpose:
- Ethical hacking is performed to identify and address security weaknesses before malicious hackers can exploit them for malicious purposes.
- The process aims to evaluate the effectiveness of an organization's security measures, policies, and controls.

2. Scope:

- Ethical hacking covers a wide range of cybersecurity assessments, including network penetration testing, web application testing, social engineering, wireless security assessments, and more.

3. Roles and Responsibilities:
- Ethical hackers are skilled cybersecurity professionals who use their expertise to identify vulnerabilities and potential attack vectors.
- The organization being tested provides the necessary authorization, cooperation, and access to conduct the assessment.

4. Methodology:
- Ethical hacking follows a structured approach, including reconnaissance, scanning, exploitation, and reporting.
- The process involves actively attempting to breach security defenses while adhering to predefined rules of engagement.

5. Reporting:

- Ethical hackers provide detailed reports on vulnerabilities discovered, along with suggested remediation measures.
- The reports help organizations understand their security gaps and prioritize the necessary improvements.

6. Legal and Ethical Considerations:
- Ethical hacking must always be conducted with proper authorization from the organization being tested.
- The ethical hacker must follow legal and ethical guidelines to protect the confidentiality, integrity, and privacy of the organization's data during the assessment.

7. Certification:
- There are various ethical hacking certifications available, such as Certified Ethical Hacker (CEH) and Offensive Security Certified Professional (OSCP), which validate the skills and knowledge of ethical hackers.

Benefits of Ethical Hacking:

- Helps organizations identify and fix security vulnerabilities before they are exploited by malicious actors.
- Provides insights into potential security risks and weaknesses in the organization's systems and processes.
- Enhances the overall security posture of an organization, reducing the likelihood of successful cyber-attacks.
- Demonstrates a proactive approach to cybersecurity, instilling confidence in customers, partners, and stakeholders.

Ethical hacking plays a vital role in modern cybersecurity practices, enabling organizations to stay one step ahead of cyber threats and protect their digital assets from potential harm.

8.2 Penetration Testing Methodologies

Penetration testing methodologies are systematic approaches used by cybersecurity professionals to conduct comprehensive and effective penetration tests. These methodologies guide the process of identifying and exploiting vulnerabilities in systems, networks, applications, and other digital assets. Different methodologies may have variations in their steps, but they generally follow a structured and repeatable process. Here are some common penetration testing methodologies:

1. Open Source Security Testing Methodology Manual (OSSTMM):
- The OSSTMM is a comprehensive methodology that focuses on security testing from a business risk perspective.
- It emphasizes identifying vulnerabilities and potential weaknesses while considering the potential impact on business operations.

2. Information Systems Security Assessment Framework (ISSAF):

- ISSAF is a structured methodology that guides testers through the various stages of a penetration test, including pre-engagement, intelligence gathering, and post-exploitation activities.
- It encompasses both technical and non-technical aspects of security assessments.

3. Open Web Application Security Project (OWASP) Testing Guide:
- The OWASP Testing Guide is specifically designed for web application security testing.
- It provides detailed guidance on identifying and remediating vulnerabilities commonly found in web applications.

4. NIST Special Publication 800-115:
- Issued by the National Institute of Standards and Technology (NIST), this publication provides guidelines for

conducting information security assessments and penetration tests.

5. Penetration Testing Execution Standard (PTES):
- PTES is a comprehensive, industry-neutral methodology that covers all aspects of penetration testing, including planning, reconnaissance, vulnerability analysis, exploitation, post-exploitation, and reporting.

6. Rapid7's Metasploit Unleashed:
- Metasploit Unleashed is a free online training course that covers the usage of the Metasploit Framework for penetration testing.

7. SANS Penetration Testing Framework:
- SANS offers a structured framework for penetration testing, including steps such as pre-engagement, intelligence gathering, vulnerability analysis, exploitation, and post-exploitation.

8. TrustedSec's Social Engineering
Framework (SEF):
- SEF focuses on social engineering
assessments and helps testers identify and
address human-related security risks.

Each of these methodologies follows a
defined sequence of steps to ensure a
comprehensive and methodical approach to
penetration testing. While performing
penetration tests, ethical hackers use a
combination of automated tools and manual
techniques to identify vulnerabilities, exploit
them, and provide actionable
recommendations to enhance the
organization's cybersecurity defenses. The
choice of the methodology may depend on
the specific objectives of the test, the nature
of the target system, and the organization's
requirements.

8.3 Exploiting Vulnerabilities and Vulnerability Assessment

Exploiting vulnerabilities and vulnerability assessment are two critical aspects of cybersecurity, especially in the context of penetration testing and improving overall security posture. Let's explore each of these concepts:

1. Exploiting Vulnerabilities:
- Exploiting vulnerabilities involves taking advantage of security weaknesses or flaws in systems, networks, applications, or devices to gain unauthorized access or control over them.
- Ethical hackers or penetration testers may exploit vulnerabilities as part of authorized assessments to demonstrate the potential impact of these weaknesses and highlight the urgency of remediation.
- The goal is to identify vulnerabilities before malicious actors do and help organizations fix them to prevent potential cyber-attacks.

- It is essential to conduct exploitation ethically and with proper authorization to avoid causing harm or violating any laws or regulations.

2. Vulnerability Assessment:

- Vulnerability assessment is a systematic process of identifying and evaluating security vulnerabilities in systems, networks, or applications.
- It involves using automated scanning tools or manual techniques to discover potential weaknesses, such as misconfigurations, software bugs, or outdated software.
- The assessment provides a snapshot of the organization's security posture and identifies areas that require immediate attention to improve security.
- Vulnerability assessments help organizations prioritize remediation efforts and proactively address potential risks before they can be exploited.

Key Differences:

- Exploiting vulnerabilities involves actively using the identified weaknesses to gain unauthorized access or control, whereas vulnerability assessment focuses on identifying vulnerabilities without actively exploiting them.
- Exploiting vulnerabilities is typically performed as part of penetration testing or ethical hacking engagements, while vulnerability assessments are more commonly used as a part of regular security assessments and compliance activities.
- Exploitation requires explicit authorization and consent from the organization being tested, while vulnerability assessments can be conducted with permission or as part of routine security monitoring.

8.4 Reporting and Mitigating Security Findings

Reporting and mitigating security findings are crucial steps in the cybersecurity process to address vulnerabilities and weaknesses identified during assessments or incident response. Both activities are essential to ensure that security risks are adequately addressed, and the organization's overall cybersecurity posture is improved. Let's delve into each of these steps:

1. Reporting Security Findings:

- Comprehensive Report: Prepare a detailed report that includes a summary of the security assessment or incident response findings. The report should be clear, concise, and tailored to the intended audience.

- Vulnerabilities Identified: Clearly list all vulnerabilities, weaknesses, and potential risks discovered during the assessment or incident investigation. Include the severity, impact, and likelihood of exploitation for each finding.

- Root Cause Analysis: Provide a root cause analysis for each vulnerability to understand the underlying reasons for their existence.

- Recommendations: Include actionable and prioritized recommendations to mitigate or remediate the identified security issues. These recommendations should be specific, feasible, and aligned with the organization's risk tolerance.

- Risk Analysis: Conduct a risk analysis to help stakeholders understand the potential impact of each security finding and make informed decisions regarding risk treatment.

- Evidence and Proof of Concept: Provide evidence, such as logs, screenshots, or step-by-step proof of concept, to demonstrate the existence and exploitability of vulnerabilities.

- Executive Summary: Create an executive summary that highlights the most critical findings and their potential impact on the organization's business operations and reputation.

- Timeline and Milestones: Set clear timelines and milestones for addressing the identified security issues to track progress and ensure timely remediation.

2. Mitigating Security Findings:

- Patching and Remediation: Apply security patches, updates, and fixes to address software vulnerabilities promptly. Keep the software and systems up to date with the latest security updates.

- Configuration Management: Review and adjust system configurations to align with security best practices, ensuring that default settings are changed, unnecessary services are disabled, and access controls are properly configured.

- Access Control: Strengthen access controls by implementing the principle of least privilege and ensuring that only authorized users have access to critical resources.

- Security Awareness Training: Conduct security awareness training for employees to educate them about common security risks, phishing attacks, and safe online practices.

- Network Segmentation: Segment networks to limit the lateral movement of attackers in case of a successful breach.

- Incident Response Plan: Develop and implement an incident response plan that outlines how the organization will respond to security incidents promptly and effectively.

- Continuous Monitoring: Implement continuous security monitoring to detect and respond to security threats in real-time.

- Penetration Testing: Regularly conduct penetration testing and vulnerability assessments to proactively identify and address security weaknesses.

- Third-Party Risk Management: Evaluate and manage the security risks posed by third-party vendors and partners that have access to critical data or systems.

Module 9: Cybersecurity for Internet of Things (IoT)

9.1 IoT Architecture and Security Challenges

IoT (Internet of Things) architecture refers to the structure and components of interconnected devices that communicate with each other and the cloud to collect, analyze, and share data. While IoT offers numerous benefits in terms of automation, efficiency, and convenience, it also introduces unique security challenges due to its vast and diverse ecosystem of connected devices. Here's an overview of IoT architecture and some of the key security challenges:

IoT Architecture Components:

1. Devices: These are the physical IoT devices, such as sensors, actuators, smart appliances, wearables, and industrial machines, which gather data and interact with the physical world.

2. Connectivity: IoT devices typically communicate through various communication protocols, such as Wi-Fi,

Bluetooth, Zigbee, cellular networks, or LoRaWAN, to transfer data to the cloud or other devices.

3. Cloud: IoT data is often processed and stored in the cloud, where it can be analyzed and accessed by applications and users.

4. Gateway: In some cases, a gateway is used to manage communication between IoT devices and the cloud, providing additional security and protocol translation.

Security Challenges in IoT Architecture:

1. Vulnerable Devices: Many IoT devices have limited resources and lack robust security features, making them susceptible to exploitation and compromise.

2. Insecure Communication: Weak or unencrypted communication channels between devices and the cloud can expose data to interception or tampering.

3. Data Privacy: The vast amount of sensitive data collected by IoT devices, such as personal information or critical infrastructure data, raises concerns about data privacy and potential data breaches.

4. Device Authentication: Ensuring secure authentication and authorization mechanisms for IoT devices is challenging, as many devices may not have the processing power or memory for complex cryptographic operations.

5. Firmware Updates and Patch Management: Updating and patching IoT device firmware is essential to address security vulnerabilities, but this process can be challenging due to device diversity and the risk of device bricking.

6. Physical Security: IoT devices in the physical world are susceptible to physical tampering, theft, or unauthorized access.

7. Lack of Standards: The lack of uniform security standards for IoT devices and communication protocols makes it difficult to establish consistent security measures across the ecosystem.

8. Scalability: As the number of IoT devices grows exponentially, managing and securing the vast network becomes increasingly complex.

Addressing IoT Security Challenges:

- Implement strong device authentication and secure communication protocols.
- Regularly update and patch IoT device firmware.
- Encrypt data at rest and in transit.
- Implement access controls and proper user authentication mechanisms.
- Use secure boot and hardware-based security features where possible.

- Conduct security testing, including penetration testing and vulnerability assessments.
- Monitor network traffic and device behavior for anomalies.
- Establish security standards and certifications for IoT devices.
- Develop a comprehensive incident response plan to address security breaches promptly.

9.2 Securing IoT Devices and Communications

Securing IoT devices and communications is critical to protect sensitive data, maintain user privacy, and prevent unauthorized access and control. As IoT devices are often resource-constrained and may lack robust security features, it's essential to implement a comprehensive security strategy that covers both the devices and the communication channels. Here are some important measures to secure IoT devices and communications:

Securing IoT Devices:

1. Secure Boot and Firmware Integrity: Implement secure boot mechanisms to ensure that only authorized and digitally signed firmware can be loaded during device boot-up.
2. Strong Device Authentication: Use strong authentication mechanisms, such as asymmetric cryptography and digital certificates, to authenticate IoT devices and prevent unauthorized access.

3. Access Control: Enforce strict access control policies to restrict device access based on user roles and privileges. Limit administrative access to only authorized personnel.

4. Encryption: Encrypt sensitive data stored on the device and data transmitted between

devices and the cloud or other devices to protect it from eavesdropping and tampering.

Securing IoT Communications:

1. Encryption: Use strong encryption protocols such as TLS (Transport Layer Security) to encrypt data transmitted over communication channels, ensuring data confidentiality and integrity.

2. Secure Protocols: Choose secure communication protocols that have undergone rigorous security assessments and avoid using outdated or vulnerable protocols.

3. Secure Key Management: Implement secure key management practices to protect encryption keys and prevent unauthorized access to sensitive data.

4. Mutual Authentication: Enable mutual authentication between devices and the cloud/server to ensure that both parties can verify each other's identity before exchanging data.

5. Virtual Private Networks (VPNs): Consider using VPNs to create secure tunnels between IoT devices and the cloud or backend systems, especially when devices communicate over untrusted networks.

9.3 Privacy and Data Protection in IoT

Privacy and data protection are crucial considerations in the context of IoT (Internet of Things) due to the extensive collection, processing, and sharing of personal and sensitive data by interconnected devices. As IoT devices become more pervasive in various domains like healthcare, smart homes, and industrial settings, ensuring the privacy of individuals and protecting their data becomes paramount. Here are key aspects related to privacy and data protection in IoT:

1. Data Minimization: Limit the collection and storage of personal data to the minimum necessary for the intended purpose. Avoid unnecessary data gathering to reduce privacy risks.

2. Informed Consent: Obtain clear and explicit consent from users before collecting their personal data. Users should be fully informed about the types of data collected, the purposes of collection, and any third-party sharing.

3. Anonymization and Pseudonymization: Whenever possible, use techniques like anonymization or pseudonymization to protect individual identities while still allowing data analysis for legitimate purposes.

4. Data Encryption: Apply strong encryption measures to protect data both at rest and in transit to prevent unauthorized access and ensure data confidentiality.

5. Secure Communication: Ensure that data transmitted between IoT devices and cloud servers or other endpoints is transmitted securely using robust encryption protocols like TLS.

6. Secure Authentication: Implement strong authentication mechanisms for IoT devices to prevent unauthorized access and protect user data from being exposed or tampered with.

7. User Access Controls: Provide users with granular control over their data, allowing them to manage permissions and revoke data access if desired.

8. Regular Security Updates: Regularly update IoT devices with security patches to

address vulnerabilities and protect against potential data breaches.

9. Secure IoT Ecosystem: Establish a secure end-to-end IoT ecosystem, including secure communication, secure device management, and secure cloud infrastructure.

10. Secure Data Storage: Ensure that data collected by IoT devices is securely stored and protected against unauthorized access or data leaks.

Protecting privacy and data in IoT requires a comprehensive approach that involves manufacturers, developers, service providers, and users working together to build a secure and privacy-aware IoT ecosystem. Adhering to privacy principles and data protection best practices will help build trust with users and maintain the privacy rights of individuals in an increasingly connected world.

9.4 IoT Security Best Practices

IoT (Internet of Things) security is critical to protect devices, data, and users from potential cyber threats and privacy breaches. Implementing best practices for IoT security helps organizations build a strong defense against malicious actors and ensures a safe and reliable IoT ecosystem. Here are some IoT security best practices:

1. Secure Device Authentication:
- Implement strong device authentication mechanisms to ensure that only authorized and trusted devices can connect to the IoT network.

2. Use Encryption:
- Employ end-to-end encryption to secure data transmission between IoT devices,

gateways, and the cloud, ensuring data confidentiality and integrity.

3. Regularly Update Firmware:
- Keep IoT device firmware and software up to date by applying security patches and updates to address known vulnerabilities.

4. Implement Access Controls:
- Enforce strict access controls to limit access to critical functions and data. Use the principle of least privilege to ensure users and devices only have the necessary permissions.

5. Secure Communication Protocols:
- Choose secure communication protocols such as TLS (Transport Layer Security) to safeguard data during transmission.

6. Conduct Security Testing:
- Regularly perform security testing, including penetration testing and

vulnerability assessments, to identify and address potential weaknesses.

7. Monitor and Analyze Network Traffic:
- Use network monitoring tools to detect abnormal behavior and potential security incidents in real-time.

8. Secure Boot and Trusted Platform Module (TPM):
- Implement secure boot mechanisms to ensure the device's integrity during startup. Use TPMs to protect cryptographic keys and perform secure operations.

9. Segment Networks:
- Segment IoT devices into separate networks to isolate them from critical systems and limit lateral movement in case of a breach.

10. Privacy by Design:

- Incorporate privacy considerations into the design and development of IoT devices and services to protect user data.

Module 10: Cybersecurity Governance and Compliance

10.1 Creating Cybersecurity Policies and Procedures

Creating cybersecurity governance and compliance involves establishing a structured framework and implementing policies and procedures to ensure that an organization's cybersecurity practices align with industry standards, regulations, and best practices. Effective cybersecurity governance and compliance measures help mitigate risks, protect sensitive data, and demonstrate a commitment to maintaining a strong security posture. Here's a step-by-step guide to creating cybersecurity governance and compliance:

1. Establish a Cybersecurity Governance Framework:

- Define Objectives: Identify the organization's cybersecurity objectives, taking into account its industry, size, and risk profile.

- Create a Cybersecurity Committee: Form a dedicated cybersecurity committee or appoint a Chief Information Security Officer (CISO) to oversee cybersecurity strategy and implementation.

- Board Involvement: Involve the board of directors in cybersecurity governance to ensure that cybersecurity is treated as a priority at the highest level.

- Risk Assessment: Conduct a comprehensive risk assessment to identify potential threats, vulnerabilities, and their potential impact on the organization.

2. Develop Cybersecurity Policies and Procedures:

- Policy Development: Create a set of cybersecurity policies that address various aspects of security, such as access control, data protection, incident response, and employee training.

- Compliance with Regulations: Ensure that cybersecurity policies align with relevant industry regulations, such as GDPR, HIPAA, or PCI DSS, if applicable to the organization.

- Incident Response Plan: Develop an incident response plan that outlines the steps to be taken in the event of a cybersecurity incident, including notification procedures and responsibilities.

- Data Protection: Establish data protection policies to safeguard sensitive information and ensure compliance with data privacy laws.

- Vendor Management: Implement guidelines for vetting and managing third-party vendors and service providers that have access to the organization's systems or data.

3. Implement Security Controls:

- Implement Cybersecurity Controls: Deploy appropriate security controls, such as firewalls, antivirus software, encryption, and multifactor authentication, to protect against common threats.

- Network Segmentation: Segment the network to limit the impact of a potential breach and prevent lateral movement of attackers.

- Regular Security Testing: Conduct periodic security testing, including vulnerability assessments and penetration testing, to identify and address weaknesses proactively.

4. Cybersecurity Awareness Training:

- Employee Training: Provide regular cybersecurity awareness training to all employees to educate them about potential threats and best practices for secure behavior.

- Phishing Awareness: Specifically address phishing and social engineering risks to prevent employees from falling victim to such attacks.

5. Continuous Monitoring and Reporting:

- Security Monitoring: Implement continuous security monitoring to detect and respond to potential security incidents in real-time.

- Incident Reporting: Establish a clear process for reporting security incidents to relevant stakeholders and regulatory authorities, as required.

6. Regular Audits and Compliance Assessments:

- Conduct Regular Audits: Perform regular cybersecurity audits to evaluate the effectiveness of security controls and ensure compliance with policies and regulations.

- Compliance Assessments: Assess the organization's compliance with relevant cybersecurity regulations and standards to identify areas for improvement.

7. Incident Response and Remediation:

- Incident Handling: Develop a clear incident response plan and designate a team responsible for coordinating and executing incident response activities.

- Post-Incident Analysis: Conduct post-incident analysis to identify lessons learned and implement improvements to prevent similar incidents in the future.

8. Review and Improve:

- Continuous Improvement: Regularly review and update cybersecurity governance and compliance measures to adapt to evolving threats and technologies.

- Collaboration and Learning: Engage with industry peers and cybersecurity communities to learn from their experiences and share knowledge.

Creating a robust cybersecurity governance and compliance program requires collaboration across departments, a commitment to continuous improvement, and a proactive approach to addressing cybersecurity risks. It is essential to adapt to changing cybersecurity landscapes and stay informed about emerging threats and best practices.

10.2 Compliance with Industry Regulations (e.g., GDPR, HIPAA)

Compliance with industry regulations, such as GDPR (General Data Protection Regulation) and HIPAA (Health Insurance Portability and Accountability Act), is crucial for organizations that handle sensitive data. These regulations impose specific requirements and standards to protect the privacy, security, and rights of individuals' personal information and healthcare data. Here are key steps to ensure compliance with GDPR and HIPAA:

1. Understand Applicability:
- Determine whether your organization is subject to GDPR or HIPAA based on the types of data you process and the industry you operate in.

2. Conduct a Data Inventory:
- Identify and document all personal data and protected health information (PHI) your organization collects, processes, and stores.

3. Define Legal Basis and Consent:
- Establish a lawful basis for processing personal data under GDPR and obtain explicit consent from individuals, if required. For HIPAA, ensure that you have the necessary authorizations for PHI use and disclosure.

4. Appoint Data Protection Officer (DPO):
- If required by GDPR, appoint a Data Protection Officer responsible for overseeing data protection practices and compliance.

5. Privacy Policy and Notices:
- Create clear and transparent privacy policies and notices that inform individuals about the data you collect, how you use it, and their rights.

6. Data Subject Rights:
- Comply with individuals' rights, such as the right to access, rectify, erase, and restrict processing of their data under GDPR.

7. Implement Security Measures:
- Adopt technical and organizational security measures to protect personal data and PHI from unauthorized access, disclosure, or breaches.

8. Conduct Risk Assessments:
- Perform risk assessments to identify and address potential vulnerabilities and data security risks.

9. Data Breach Response:

- Develop and practice a data breach response plan to promptly detect, report, and respond to data breaches, as required by GDPR and HIPAA.

10. Vendor Management:
- Ensure that any third-party vendors or business associates handling personal data or PHI are compliant with the regulations.

11. Employee Training:
- Provide regular training to employees on GDPR and HIPAA requirements, data handling best practices, and the importance of data privacy.

12. Data Retention and Disposal:
- Establish policies for data retention and secure disposal of data when it is no longer needed, complying with regulatory requirements.

13. Audit and Monitoring:

- Regularly audit and monitor your data processing activities and security measures to ensure ongoing compliance.

14. Record Keeping:
- Maintain accurate records of data processing activities, data subject requests, and security incidents.

15. Regular Compliance Reviews:
- Conduct periodic compliance reviews and assessments to verify that your organization adheres to GDPR and HIPAA requirements.

Compliance with GDPR and HIPAA demonstrates a commitment to protecting data privacy and security, fostering trust with customers and stakeholders. Organizations must stay up-to-date with regulatory changes and adapt their practices to meet evolving compliance requirements. Additionally, seeking legal counsel or data protection experts can provide valuable guidance to ensure full compliance with these complex regulations.

10.3 Cybersecurity Audits and Risk Assessment

Cybersecurity audits and risk assessments are critical components of a proactive cybersecurity strategy. They help organizations identify security weaknesses, assess potential risks, and take measures to protect their systems, data, and assets. Let's explore each of these practices:

1. Cybersecurity Audits:

Cybersecurity audits involve a comprehensive and systematic evaluation of an organization's cybersecurity policies, procedures, controls, and practices. The primary goal of a cybersecurity audit is to assess the effectiveness of an organization's security measures and identify areas for improvement. Here's how cybersecurity audits are conducted:

- Scope Definition: Determine the scope of the audit, including the systems, networks, applications, and processes to be assessed.

- Examination of Controls: Review existing security controls and measures to ensure they align with industry best practices, regulations, and internal policies.

- Vulnerability Assessment: Conduct vulnerability assessments and penetration tests to identify potential weaknesses and security gaps.

- Compliance Verification: Verify compliance with relevant regulations, standards, and internal security policies.

- Incident Response Evaluation: Assess the organization's incident response capabilities and preparedness to handle security incidents.

- Risk Assessment: Evaluate the organization's risk posture and identify high-risk areas that require immediate attention.

- Reporting: Produce a detailed audit report that highlights findings, vulnerabilities, compliance status, and recommendations for improvement.

2. Risk Assessment:

A risk assessment is a structured process of identifying, analyzing, and evaluating potential risks and their impact on an organization's assets, operations, and objectives. It helps organizations prioritize their security efforts and allocate resources effectively. Here's how risk assessments are conducted:

- Asset Identification: Identify and document all critical assets, such as data, systems, applications, and physical infrastructure.

- Threat Identification: Identify potential threats and risks that could exploit vulnerabilities and impact the organization's assets.

- Vulnerability Assessment: Conduct a vulnerability assessment to determine the organization's exposure to potential security weaknesses.

- Risk Analysis: Analyze the likelihood and potential impact of identified risks on the organization.

- Risk Evaluation: Evaluate the identified risks based on their severity and prioritize them based on the level of potential impact.

- Risk Mitigation: Develop and implement risk mitigation strategies to reduce the likelihood or impact of identified risks.

- Continuous Monitoring: Continuously monitor the risk landscape and update risk assessments as new threats and vulnerabilities emerge.

By regularly conducting cybersecurity audits and risk assessments, organizations can gain insights into their security posture, identify areas for improvement, and proactively address potential security risks. These practices help organizations build a robust cybersecurity framework, minimize security breaches, and protect their sensitive data and digital assets.

10.4 Cybersecurity Incident Handling and Reporting

Cybersecurity incident handling and reporting are critical processes to effectively respond to and manage security incidents in an organization. The primary objective is to minimize the impact of incidents, protect sensitive data, and restore normal operations as quickly as possible. Here are the key steps involved in incident handling and reporting:

1. Incident Identification and Classification:

- Establish Incident Categories: Define incident categories based on their severity and potential impact on the organization's operations and data.

- Incident Detection: Use security monitoring tools and proactive threat hunting to identify potential security incidents promptly.

2. Incident Response Team Activation:

- Assemble an Incident Response Team (IRT): Form a dedicated team with representatives from IT, security, legal, management, and relevant stakeholders to handle the incident.

- Designate Incident Response Roles: Assign specific roles and responsibilities within the IRT, such as incident coordinator, technical experts, and communication liaison.

3. Incident Containment and Eradication:

- Contain the Incident: Take immediate actions to isolate the affected systems, networks, or devices to prevent further spread of the incident.

- Eradicate the Threat: Determine the root cause of the incident and remove the malicious elements from the affected systems.

4. Data Collection and Preservation:

- Preserve Evidence: Ensure that all evidence related to the incident is collected and preserved properly to support further investigation and potential legal actions.

- Document Incident Details: Thoroughly document all actions taken during the incident response process, including timestamps, findings, and remediation steps.

5. Incident Analysis and Impact Assessment:

- Investigate the Incident: Conduct a detailed analysis of the incident to understand its scope, impact, and extent of data compromise.

- Impact Assessment: Evaluate the potential consequences of the incident on the organization's operations, reputation, and compliance.

6. Incident Communication and Reporting:

- Internal Communication: Keep all relevant stakeholders, including executives, IT teams, and affected personnel, informed about the incident's status and response actions.

- External Reporting: Comply with any legal or regulatory requirements for incident reporting, which may involve notifying law enforcement or data protection authorities.

7. Incident Recovery and Lessons Learned:

- Incident Recovery: Implement necessary measures to restore affected systems, applications, and data to normal functioning.

- Post-Incident Review: Conduct a thorough post-incident review to identify lessons learned and areas for improvement in incident response procedures.

8. Continuous Improvement:

- Update Incident Response Plans: Incorporate lessons learned from incidents into incident response plans to enhance the organization's incident handling capabilities.

- Ongoing Monitoring: Continuously monitor the organization's security infrastructure to detect and respond to potential future incidents promptly.

By following a well-defined incident handling process and promptly reporting incidents, organizations can effectively mitigate the impact of security breaches and improve their overall cybersecurity resilience. Incident handling and reporting are essential components of a proactive cybersecurity strategy that helps protect against evolving cyber threats.